FORTUNE
AND
FAME

Jonathan Power

Print ISBN 9780957245969

The right of Jonathan Power to be identified as the author of this
work has been asserted by him in accordance with the Copyright
Designs and Patents Act 1988

Published by
Llyfrau Cambria Books, Wales, United Kingdom.
Cambria Books is a division of
Cambria Publishing Ltd.

Discover our other books at: www.cambriabooks.co.uk

Dedication

For my Parents

You taught me to make the opportunities.

Without you, this story would never have happened.

I am delighted that my book will be supporting our official charity Velindre Fundraising, and 10% of all book profits will be donated.

JP

Acknowledgements

This book is a roadmap of my professional achievements and the path that I have followed to earn my success. I hope you are inspired by my journey.

My story is one of commitment, dedication and relationship building, and introduces the remarkable personalities I encountered along the way.

Throughout my career, I have been blessed to meet a variety of unique and wonderful people, and have collaborated with some of the greatest names from the world of sport and entertainment.

As their representative and advisor, I was centre stage in their professional associations, and yes, I occasionally shared in their glory. The trappings of my success arose from the strength of the solid relationships I was able to establish, and it was my privilege to collaborate with them all. They have made the tale worth telling.

I also want to pay tribute to the staff who worked so tirelessly behind the scenes in delivering our services to clients. My thanks also to the business associates and advisors whose names feature throughout these pages.

I especially want to recognise the small and dedicated team who have helped deliver this book.

To Chris Jones and everyone at Cambria for backing the potential of Fortune and Fame. Their faith, support and guidance have been immeasurable. Thanks also to Sophie Johnson, Annalisa Jones and Margaret Harlin for their invaluable and wide-ranging assistance.

I am also incredibly grateful and honoured to have as part of my team, the "artist to the stars" Nathan Wyburn. Nathan created and designed the unique front cover for this book. Thank you for believing in the project Nathan.

To my good friend David Collins, whose skills and experience as a writer and journalist played such a big part in helping to deliver this project.

You have all been critical to the production of my story.

Finally, to my girls. My wife Emma and my lovely daughter Millie. You were there for the highs and the lows. You endured the tough times and shared in the rewards. You are the power behind The Power.

Thanks girls. x

Foreword

Jonathan, I met him some years ago when I was still playing football and he helped me with some very shrewd business advice with quite a few properties.

I only wished I had stayed in touch with him regarding the advice that he had given me.

Some years later I came across Jonathan again and wow, that's all I can say, as what he did for me when I caught up with him again has changed my life in a way that I will always be indebted to him - for his honesty and his help.

Andrew Cole
187 Premier League Goals

Prologue

Believe in yourself.

Aim for the stars. Work hard, work smart and work even harder again. There is no shortcut to achieving success. Never give up.

Anything is possible and remember, ambition has no ceiling.

Or you could just sit back, relax, and aim low. You'd never be disappointed.

Jonathan Power 2022

CONTENTS

Poster Boy

Some individuals achieve such fame for their contribution to history, that they are capable of identification by just a single name.

Churchill. Hitler. Stalin.

Shakespeare. Mozart. Elvis.

Such recognition may reflect their achievements, notoriety, talent, or all the above.

Their names enter the lexicon of a nation.

JFK. Nixon. Lennon & McCartney. Titles that evoke the lives and legacy of the personnel concerned.

It crops up in sports frequently. Torvill & Dean. McEnroe. KP.

The famous Welsh rugby stars of the 70s are still often referred to by their Christian names alone in the South Wales Valleys. Even by just their initials. JPR is known to all. 'Alun Wyn' has continued the trend.

It is especially common in football.

Beckenbauer. Beckham. Shearer.

Matthews. Finney. Gazza.

Who was better: Ronaldo or Messi? History will deliberate on that one for decades.

The single names of Best, Charlton & Law define an entire soccer dynasty.

Sir Alex.

Moore, Peters, and Hurst will remain English heroes forever.

Sir Alf.

Perhaps though, it crops up most often in boxing.

Ali v Frazier.

Bruno. AJ. Marciano for older readers. Calzaghe. Tyson.

Tyson.

Mike Tyson is one of those figures whose fame surpasses his own world. Undoubtedly one of the fiercest heavyweight boxers of all time, his list of achievements makes impressive reading. Winning his first 19 fights by knockout. Unification of world titles. Awesome achievements in his early twenties.

Tyson's reputation defined him. Victory over Michael Spinks in 91 seconds, knocking out the legendary Larry Holmes, demolishing all-comers with chilling ruthlessness. Simple black shorts. Cold eyes and a hammer in each hand. A fighter who cared little for the more refined niceties of the noble art.

At the height of his fame, the softly spoken Tyson was, quite simply, one of the most recognised sporting personalities in the whole world. In addition to his many accomplishments in the ring though, his activities on the other side of the ropes also kept him firmly in the public eye

His first wife, Robin Givens, described living with him as "torture, pure hell, worse than anything I could possibly imagine." Some stories claim that he made a prison official pregnant while in jail; that he wrestled with a tiger and that he even offered a member of staff at a zoo $10,000 to let him fight a gorilla. Tyson apparently offered the sum to a zookeeper in the hope that he'd let him fight a silverback gorilla. The legendary former heavyweight champion has told the story of how his offer was declined on a day he'd hired out the entire zoo just for him and Robin Givens. Unsurprisingly the fight never took place.

Tyson's intimidating, all-embracing face tattoos seem mild in comparison, don't they?

So, yes, my meeting with Iron Mike Tyson remains fixed in my mind.

My rendezvous with him came about through my association with Welsh boxer Joe Calzaghe.

By the time Joe's details appeared in my phone book, I was already well established, providing independent financial and investment advice to a growing list of household names, especially from the world of sport and entertainment.

Joe though, Joe was something else. To the outside world, his name may not trip readily off the tongue in any list of the world's greatest pugilists. History though will prove otherwise.

I began my association with Joe not long after he defeated legendary British boxer, Chris Eubank, for the vacant WBO Super-Middleweight Championship in 1997 in Sheffield. Eubank later described the Welsh ace as the "proper article, a true warrior."

Despite his Hammersmith origins, Joe wore his mother's Welshness with pride, emerging as an icon of the 'Cool Cymru' brand (*Cymru = Wales in Welsh*) that emerged to embrace stars such as Catatonia, the Manic Street Preachers, and others during the 90s. The Juventus-supporting boxer held world championships at two weights, including the unified WBA (Super), WBC, IBF, WBO, *Ring Magazine* and lineal super-middleweight titles, and the *Ring* light-heavyweight title. He is the longest reigning super-middleweight world champion in boxing history, having held the WBO title for over 10 years. Joe retired with the longest continual stint as the world champion of any active fighter at the time. He was also the first man to unify three of the four major world titles (WBA, WBC, and WBO) at super- middleweight, and was the first *Ring* champion in that weight class. Rare blemishes on his career had been a 1990 defeat at the hands of another of my clients, Michael Smythe, at the Welsh ABA finals and Romanian Adrian Opreda at the 1990 European Junior Championships in Prague. This had still left Joe with an impressive 110–10 record as an amateur mind. His professional career finished with 46 fights, and 46 wins. That's only three less than Rocky Marciano.

So yes, Joe has some standing within boxing circles and entered the Boxing Hall of Fame in 2014. He also collected the *BBC Sports Personality of the Year Award* in 2007. Joe has been awarded the title of *Welsh Sports Personality of the Year* three times.

Over the years, as with many of my clients, I became not just Joe's advisor but also his representative, advocate, and confidant.

3

"Mates" even.

I also advised Joe's Italian-born father, Enzo. Famous names.

Tyson though, Tyson's fame was simply on another level again.

Joe Calzaghe was due to meet David Starie at the MEN Arena, Manchester on 29 January 2000. At the time, Joe was the WBO Super-Middleweight champion. World Champion. 27 undefeated contests to date. Top billing, you might think.

One MG Tyson was also set to appear on the card, however. A gift for the media men and publicity machinery.

Even though the fearsome Tyson's best results occurred long before entering the ring that night in Manchester, the Tyson legend remained pure box office. His notoriety and past achievements still ensured bums on seats, irrespective of his faded glory. The tune may have been over but the malady lingered on.

Tyson was set to share the ring with Julius Francis, a 35-year-old Londoner whose modest achievements to date had included gaining a coveted Lonsdale Belt, a reward bestowed on fighters who had won three British title fights.

This was to be Tyson's 51st professional bout but his first in the UK. His list of earlier conquests reads like a 'who's who' of the noble art. Bruno, Spinks, Holmes. Chilling victories, ferocious punching, unification fights, Madison Square Garden, the Las Vegas Hilton, and Caesar's Palace. Tyson had been brought to you by HBO, Showtime, and King Vision. He had been promoted by Don King during his career – himself a controversial figure, partly due to a manslaughter conviction and civil cases against him. These guys simply don't settle for second billing.

So, it perhaps came as a little surprise to some that, even though the night marked the latest encounter for a WBO World Champion of some standing, the legendary name and persona of Mike Tyson still dominated the build-up.

This was to be Tyson's first fight on European soil and the reputation of the New York City slugger easily preceded him into the Manchester contest.

4

Home Secretary Jack Straw granted a dispensation to Tyson – who had served half of a six-year jail sentence after being convicted of rape in 1992, before then being imprisoned again for four months in 1999 for attacking two motorists – to even enter the UK. Justice for Women, a feminist campaigning organisation, had tried to stop the fighter's entry into the country.

None of this fazed Iron Mike of course as the native New Yorker's entourage took over an entire floor of London's Grosvenor House Hotel. Chaotic scenes at Heathrow added to the aura of menace. His visit to Brixton attracted 2,000 onlookers. There were stories of a shopping spree that saw him spend £450,000 on high-end jewellery.

As an aside, this occasion also includes a bizarre story in the lead-up to the fight.

Francis approached me for independent, financial advice via his agent, with whom I had already established a strong business relationship. I never formalised an arrangement with him though I was able to help him out a little when I spent a few hours in conversation with him.

Francis also saw that the bout with the legendary Tyson provided him with a unique opportunity to maximise his earnings. He reported, "I got paid £350,000 for the fight, while Tyson got £7m. I'm not annoyed about that, but people think I got a lot for it."

To boost his purse, Francis told me that he had agreed on an amazing deal with the *Daily Mirror* newspaper to have the bottom of his boxing shoes sponsored. Piers Morgan would have been a key decision maker at the *Mirror* in those times. The thinking being, I guess, that as he lay spreadeagled on the canvas courtesy of another blow from the iron fists of Mike Tyson, the entire world would believe that this fighter was an avid *Daily Mirror* reader. They would also view the *Mirror* logo in full colour of course. Marketing and commercialism at their most ruthless. You couldn't make it up, could you?

The fight itself was irrelevant. Tyson sent the underdog Francis to the canvas five times, fully justifying the *Daily*

Mirror's audacious investment, before winning the fight as early as the second round. The 17-stone, Peckham-born Francis later described how the sheer power of the punches he faced had even lifted him off the ground. Only fools & boxers, eh?

So, as I say, what with the boxing and brutality, Tyson, despite an uncertain reputation, remained a 'celebrity' to put it mildly. Fame and recognition on a global scale.

Tyson's reputation, history, and sheer magnitude even impressed our man Calzaghe in the build-up to the Manchester Massacre.

Joe came face-to-face with Tyson after his father Enzo almost provoked a fight with the so-called Baddest Man on The Planet.

Training alongside one another for a week, Calzaghe claimed he asked Tyson for a photo.

Pietro Vincenzo "Enzo" Calzaghe, Joe's dad, was charged with taking the photograph.

Enzo himself was no slouch when it came to ringside craft either mind. In recognition of his achievements as Joe's coach, he won 'Coach of the Year' at the BBC Sports Personality awards, *The Ring Magazine* trainer of the year for 2007, and the Futch–Condon Award, awarded by the Boxing Writers Association of America, for Trainer of the Year in 2007.

Enzo had been a schoolmate of Joe Bugner – who went 12 rounds with both Ali and Frazier in his time – and had learned to box to protect himself from school bullies.

But Iron Mike clearly wasn't in the mood for photographic niceties, declining to even smile for the camera.

The tough Sardinian Enzo was unimpressed by this lack of chivalry from the former world champion. He confronted the American "Are you gonna smile or what?" he enquired.

Amazingly Calzaghe Senior's head remained attached to his 5'7" frame after this exchange and Joe later joined Iron Mike for a chat outside the gym, where Tyson talked about family, money….and eating Don King's children.

My role in all of this had been largely that of a bemused

observer. I was the same height as Enzo. Extracting reluctant smiles from the Baddest Man on the Planet had not hitherto featured on my bucket list so I had stayed well out of it all.

Joe saw a role for me. Even though *he* was the world champ, the pre-fight publicity was all about Iron Mike. Publicity posters screamed the single word, 'TYSON.'

The whole world knew just who 'Tyson' was. Beneath the dayglo blue and green lettering, the unmistakable, enormous face of Tyson glared out – and no, he wasn't smiling.

Somewhere near the foot of the poster, almost as an afterthought even, promoter Frank Warren had condescended to make mention of the fact that Joe Calzaghe, incidentally, would also be fighting that night, for something called the World Championship. The picture of Joe took up almost as much space on the poster as Tyson's left ear.

Now, even though Joe Calzaghe was a world champion, a Welsh sporting icon, and a figure of some fame and fortune himself by now, he remained a boxing fan. Joe wanted Tyson to sign some posters for his children.

It's not that simple though when you are champion of the world. Especially after the photo session experience described above. Eyebrows had already been raised when Francis had reportedly asked for an autograph at the pre-fight weigh-in. Reigning world champions who have dominated all comers, simply do not hang around outside dressing rooms hoping for a chance to ask fighters on the undercard for autographs. Never mind who they are.

It may have been ok for Julius Francis but Francis was no Calzaghe. No legendary, undefeated champion.

"That's ok," thought Joe. "Jon will do it."

Will he?

This was not the first time that the Calzaghe camp had found me additional employment by the way. As Joe trained one morning, Enzo had me sit at ringside in the gym under strict instructions to ring the bell every three minutes. Presumably, this was designed to replicate the three-minute round-by-round conditions of the big fight. I sat in the corner as Enzo put Joe through his paces. As each three-minute warning arrived, I clanged the bell hard. I often performed some unusual roles for my clients though, so I simply stuck to my task. From tea boy to bell boy now.

I supported my clients throughout their careers and have enjoyed watching many of them utilise their talents at big events, usually from the best seats in the house. Enzo kindly arranged 10 ringside seats for me for the night in Manchester but, to be honest, I could have used 100. My phone never stopped ringing as international sportsmen clamoured for the chance to witness a legend in the flesh.

Watching Tyson train in that gym that he shared with Joe was a tremendous experience. His sheer, powerful force left us breathless and open-mouthed. Over the years, I worked with many great fighters – champions such as Robbie Regan, Steve Robinson, and Howard Eastman, who fought Bernard Hopkins for the World Title. This guy Tyson was a whole new ball game though. He was simply ferocious, even in training.

So, I find myself sitting later at the Grosvenor House, on Park Lane. Joe has assigned me the role of autograph hunter.

The Grosvenor is a 5-star venue within the upscale neighbourhood of Mayfair. We are moments from Hyde Park, Oxford Street, Buckingham Palace, and more.

The exclusive gathering which had assembled after training at the gym had finished, comprised me, promoter Frank Warren, the two Calzaghe Boys… and the man who had once been disqualified in a contest with Evander Holyfield in 1997 for biting Holyfield's ears. One bite notoriously being strong enough to remove a portion of his right ear. We sat for over an hour, all very relaxed, even with a heavy security presence at the door.

The Islington-born Warren was a very big player on the world boxing scene.

During his time he promoted and managed world champions and top-ranked fighters including Joe, Naseem Hamed, Frank Bruno, Tyson Fury, Nigel Benn, Chris Eubank, Amir Khan , and Ricky Hatton. He had guided Hamed to become Britain's youngest ever world champion when he overcame another of my clients, Steve Robinson, to win the WBO Featherweight title in Cardiff in 1995.

In 1989, he had been shot outside the Broadway Theatre in Barking by an unknown gunman in a balaclava. The former boxer, Terry Marsh, who had become Warren's first world champion two years earlier, was accused of the shooting but later acquitted. The Arsenal fan certainly made for an interesting guest at our table.

Joe Calzaghe had, of course, been successful in persuading me to play the part of the autograph hunter. After all, when a world champion asks a favour, it's hard to decline the request.

The after-dinner conversation reached a natural lull at one point. Here was my chance.

Reaching below the table, I quietly collected two or three of the posters. "Excuse me, Mike, would you mind signing a couple of posters please?"

The fearsome Mike Tyson glared back at me. Eyes that had sent fear into boxing greats, stared at me coldly. Ice eyes. I felt my throat dry up. This man took the word 'imposing' to new heights.

He said simply, "No." Then there was a pause. A long pause.

"I don't understand," I somehow replied. "No, you don't mind or no you won't sign them?"

What could be described as a stand-off then followed as the fearsome Tyson glared at me. I forget the exact terms of his supplementary response now, suffice to say that it was firmly in the negative, and sprinkled with expletives. The convivial mood in the room quickly changed.

I slid the posters away. Embarrassed in front of legends. Neither of the Calzaghe boys said a word. Nor did Warren. "No" had simply been enough for them.

As we were all shocked and ill-prepared for such behaviour, I soon made my excuses and left. In any event, I had a meeting arranged that afternoon elsewhere in the hotel with Dutch footballer Nordin Wooter. Wooter had begun his career at Ajax but was with Watford at the time. As with so many of the stars I advised over the years we had also become great friends alongside our business relationship.

In the hotel foyer later, Joe came up to me and reassured me. "It's ok man" he promised. "Mike will sign the posters, no bother." I was ready to go again. Tyson would sign the posters after the press conference Joe promised. The press conference was due to start imminently.

Power v Tyson II. The rematch. I approached the Brooklyn Bruiser for a second time.

"So, about these posters then Mike?"

The terror was cranked up. This time it was personal. Tyson stared into my eyes from a matter of inches. "Had he not told me before?"

Tyson's neck measured 20 inches in diameter. That's nearly two feet ear-to-ear. His 71" reach meant that he could have hit me from over five feet away. He was much, much closer than five feet though, believe me. A cold sweat soon occupied my brow.

I felt my own ear twitch as I glimpsed those snarling teeth. The same dentures that had munched on Holyfield. One of the most feared men in the history of sport now gave it to me both barrels. I trembled visibly. Haverfordwest had not prepared me for a confrontation such as this.

"Who the f…. What the f……. bad ass mother f…er." I had the lot. The full Brooklyn vocabulary. Eddie Murphy on speed as the giant frame of Tyson stood inches from my eyes. There was no Enzo in my corner to throw in the towel either.

So, was this how my life was to end? Mauled by a tiger wrestler in a top London hotel?

I decided that it was time to finally blow my cover.

Joe and I were pals, but I felt obliged to drop him in it now.

"It's not for me. It's for Joe, honest."

Tyson's snarling mood switched in a heartbeat. The angry man was gone. Wild eyes now smiled at me, as a friendly uncle might regard a tiny tot. A pussycat emerged. That gentle lisp soothed the savage beast and defused the enormous situation. Hyde became Jekyll. The monster is gone. What the......?

"Well, sure, if it's for Joe."

It was all "Hey Man, your name is Jon, right?"

"Well Jon, the first poster is for you."

Tyson signed the poster "To Jon from Mike Tyson." I still have it. I was his best friend now. We even had a photo taken. Tyson, Joe, and I. This time he even smiled.

I couldn't decide whether to laugh or cry.

My heart thumped evenly once more. A white-robed, scythe-carrying figure slipped away into the shadows. His time would come again. My time had not yet come.

Within seconds, Tyson had moved from likely assassin to become my best buddy. Quite a guy, eh?

Tyson.

***

So, inevitably perhaps, I hear you ask....

How did a quiet young lad from a modest upbringing in sleepy Pembrokeshire, West Wales, with no formal educational qualifications graduate to dine out with legends?

Why do Knights of the Realm, sporting superstars, and pop idols now know him by his Christian name alone? He has mixed with senior royals and establishment figures.

How on earth could he buy a luxury sports car for a six-figure sum and a six-bedroom executive home in the leafy Cardiff suburbs? He dines in 5-star hotels with international celebrities. How can *you* reach such dizzy heights?

This is the point of this book. If you aspire to reach your own potential: read on.

Sometimes, the race is not won by the swift, or the battle by the strong; but time and chance happen to them all.

Will you take that chance? *Make* that chance even?

If there was a 48-hour day and 10 days a week, would you

work them? Are you prepared to make *and* take the breaks; to make your own luck; to seize the chances that come your way?

I want to inspire you. I want you to know just what it takes. Yes, I hope you enjoy the stories, the famous names, and the superstar insights. But hey, this could be you. Honest. It really could. Maybe you won't reach the heights that I reached but, do you know…you might.

If you aspire to achieve, however modest your ambitions may be, then follow that dream. Dream on and chase your dream.

You will need hard work – inspiration and perspiration. You will need luck. You will need friends you can trust. A loving supportive family helped me, though not all can be so lucky.

Good role models can help shape you or inform your decision-making. A wise and encouraging teacher perhaps. At the end of the day though, it's down to you. No-one else.

You will need a cool head, a strong will, and good character.

You will need a backbone, a funny bone, and a wishbone.

Oh, and you might need a bike.

Pedal Power

Haverfordwest is a town in West Wales.

That's pretty much all you might know about it. All you might say about it, even.

Like most towns in Wales, it features a castle. Believed to be of twelfth-century origins, it was once held by Edward, the Black Prince. The castle later proved strong enough to rebut an attack from Owain Glyndwr, the rebellious Welsh leader from the Middle Ages.

The tidal waters of the Western Cleddau river rush past these walls, barging their way through the centre of the town on the way to Milford Haven. To see the oil refinery, I expect.

Haverfordwest and Milford Haven represent urban oddities in the largely rural, idyllic county of Pembrokeshire.

Such outposts of the UK landmass probably don't feature on your radar if you live in West Hampstead or Salford Quays. They are somewhat off the 'bucket & spade trail' of spectacular beaches, hidden coves, and coastal paths that hug the entire perimeter of this stunning and beautiful part of Wales.

Compared to the majestic, sandy wonders of Whitesands Bay or Newgale, a long weekend in Haverfordwest is unlikely to feature on too many bucket lists I imagine.

'Visit Pembrokeshire' proudly introduces Haverfordwest as an "attractive and ancient county town." We learn that it serves as the county's administrative centre, with shops and even retail parks.

Despite these metropolitan-sounding claims though, the modern population of the town totals only around 12,000. To put that into context, the capacity of Fir Park, home of Motherwell FC, is just over 13,000. The actor Christian Bale was born in Haverfordwest. Yes, that's right. Batman is from Pembrokeshire, though Gotham City is not, I am told, twinned with its county town. Shame.

In my adult life, I spent so much time in London, that I invested in a portfolio of properties, including an apartment at

Chelsea Waterside, which formed my London home.

Even with a decent car, limited toilet stops, and an uninterrupted passage through the notorious Brynglas Tunnels at Newport, it would still take some five hours to drive from Chelsea to Haverfordwest today. You could probably fly to Moscow in that time you know.

In my early days in Pembrokeshire during the mid-60s, it probably felt even further away from London centric consciousness. No M4. No Sat Nav. No Severn Bridge. It doesn't bear thinking about.

Such geographical and navigational intricacies were, of course, completely lost on me at the time. As a tot in short trousers, the mediaeval market town provided for my every need.

Located in West Wales between Milford Haven, Pembroke Dock, Fishguard , and St David's, Haverfordwest provided easy access to the beaches and countryside of Pembrokeshire. As the youngest of three brothers, my early life was a constant ritual of three-horse races, as we did our best to emulate the silky samba-soccer skills of the 1970 Brazilian World Cup side on the West Wales sands.

When the summer came, as it seemed to do more frequently back then, it was time for cricket. The surrounding beaches called for real artistry as their unforgiving sandy wickets gave little encouragement to a seven-year-old lower order batsman, swinging willow at leather until the sun went down over the surrounding Preseli hills and mountains.

Why can't life stay like this, eh?

We grew up in Coronation Avenue in the Prendergast area of Haverfordwest. It was well served by schools and local amenities. It was modest. Just enough garden space to polish those football skills or perfect the art of spin bowling.

In later years we moved to Fenton Villas. Despite sounding like an expensive South American midfield signing for Manchester City, Fenton Villas was also modest.

Although the three brothers – Dave, Colin, and I – were more than happy in such idyllic surroundings, my parents knew that there could be more to life than this. They did not relish the chances of three sons and their young daughter Margaret, achieving economic success in this quiet town on a westerly, far-flung peninsula of the British Isles. They knew that we would need help.

They knew that the opportunity needed creating. Taking. We needed to make our own luck.

Dad had a decent job back then, a managerial position with the GPO as Acting Assistant Inspector.

To those of you not raised in the black-and-white TV days of the 60s as I was, the General Post Office (GPO) was the UK state postal system. People made their views known to the outside world by putting handwritten notes into tiny paper envelopes and depositing them in large, red, metal boxes at the end of the street. The GPO would then empty the boxes and dispatch the petite packages around the country, usually by the next day. Honest.

"Happy Birthday Auntie Megan."

"Wish you were here."

"Please find enclosed cheque for...."

"Dear Sir, I believe I may have heard the first cuckoo of spring here in Solva."

Nobody took their telephone to the pub to take a photograph of their lunch back then.

No computer in your pocket so that you could share your every view with your nearest and dearest. The GPO would do that.

Really, it's extremely hard to overstate the nationwide influence of the GPO in the days before Geoff Hurst crashed in his famous hat-trick.

Mum and Dad knew though, that they needed to make changes. They also knew that choices were limited. We had to get away. They had to give the four of us the breaks.

Dad contemplated the options. The streets of London may have been paved with gold, but it would take days to even get there with four kids. Dick Whittington could have that gig he

15

decided.

Even Cardiff was 100 miles away.

Swansea? Perhaps.

My parents were not ones for games of chance but knew that fate needed to play a part here. They took out a coin.

Heads Cardiff. Tails Swansea.

The coin turned in the air.

Lives hung in the balance.

The coin landed.

"Cardiff."

Dave puffed out his cheeks. He was an avid Cardiff City fan.

The Dai was cast.

***

Do you recall the 60s US sitcom, *The Beverly Hillbillies*, about a family of country bumpkins who upped sticks and moved to California when they came into wealth?

The rough and ready family from the hills of the Ozarks, who moved to the swish environment of California, who left their rustic home with all their possessions – including Grandma on her rocking chair – piled up high on the back of their old wagon.

That wasn't quite how it was for us but it certainly echoed that scene as we left Pembrokeshire in my uncle's removal truck in 1971 heading for, well who knows what, in the long, dark streets of the capital.

Dad had managed to secure a new position at the GPO and although the position meant a demotion and a drop in salary, he knew that it could help pave the way to better opportunities for the four young Power siblings. Our mum supported dad every step of the way as we shifted on life's axis.

We all moved into uncle Reggie's house in Newport Road, Cardiff. Reg shared the large property with his family and that of another uncle, Vernon. We were the third family living in the property then. There must have been 14 of us living in that house at the time. That was just the way it was for many families. Shipped in from rural West Wales, the long, straight streets of inner Cardiff would take some getting used to. No sandy wickets here to help bowl a maiden over. Cardiff kids were into baseball, whatever that was.

Not long after we had all crammed into 'Chez Reg', a work colleague of my father managed to secure us a council house. Bill Carling was a "tough as old boots" Cardiff postal worker, with a tiny frame and huge political heart. Labour. Old Labour.

Bill somehow secured a home for us in Arran Street, Roath. No 23.

Arran Street was one of many rows of terraced housing which continue to link bustling City Road with Cottrell Road. A small garden at No 23 could just about accommodate three George Best impersonators and a reluctant sister. She was more concerned with the Bay City Rollers and David Essex than nurturing our sporting prowess though.

City Road was originally known as Castle Road but changed to City Road when Cardiff achieved city status in 1905.

This wasn't exactly the Beverly Hills landscape we had set out for, but it was at least an urban setting awash with commercial opportunities. Dad felt he had done well.

Bill Carling, incidentally, represented the tough 'council estate' ward of Ely, on the western edge of the city. It's a challenging patch, believe me. Go there. Councillor William Henry Carling represented Ely with such gusto that he eventually achieved the status of Lord Mayor in 1978. The Lord Mayor of Cardiff is actually considered to be the first citizen of Wales and since 1955, has enjoyed the title of 'Right Honourable.'

Many towns and cities have a mayor, some have a Lord Mayor but the capital of Wales is one of a select band of towns whose first citizen carries the title Rt. Hon Lord Mayor. I think it's only four or five cities that can boast that proud title.

Maybe Dad's coin had landed the right way up after all?

Whilst it may have appalled Councillor Carling, Margaret Thatcher's Tory government introduced The Right to Buy scheme for Council tenants.

After Margaret Thatcher became Prime Minister in May 1979, the legislation to implement The Right to Buy was passed by virtue of the 1980 Housing Act. Millions of people were affected by this iconic legislative development, so typical of 80s ambitions and entrepreneurship.

Environment Secretary Michael Heseltine exclaimed that "no single piece of legislation has enabled the transfer of so much capital wealth from the state to the people". He argued that the initiative had given the public what they wanted and reversed the trend of state dominance.

To what extent the ideological exuberances of the Swansea-born Heseltine reached my parents' consciousness at the time, we will never know, suffice to say, that this "can do: must do" attitude fired his imagination. As it later fired mine. It would be many years though before I convinced them that money spent on a mortgage was better business than shelling out dead money on rent.

Our new house was not far from the busy shopping terrace known as Albany Road. Large parts of inner-city Cardiff were developed and formalised during the Victorian era. Much of central Cardiff retains a remarkably similar appearance to how it looked in days gone by. Even today a night in the pubs and curry houses that surround this ancient thoroughfare is hard to beat.

Albany Road was formerly known as Merthyr Road but, in a nod to Victoriana, was renamed Albany Road in 1884 to commemorate the passing of Prince Leopold, Duke of Albany, son of Queen Victoria.

I attended Albany Road Junior School. The school was opened in November 1887 and quickly expanded to accommodate some 1600 pupils come the end of the century. The Victorian fortress was also put into use as a military hospital during WWI.

My place in the annals of the history of this academic centre of excellence was unlikely to come from my scholastic abilities. I managed to force my way into the school football team though, where I did my best to transfer my West Walian beach soccer

18

skills to the muddy playing fields of Cardiff in the 70s. We played our home games at the nearby Roath Recreation Ground and even some matches in the schoolyard.

It was during my time at Albany Road that I first developed my musical and artistic abilities. Well, that is, I played the recorder. I must have managed it reasonably well though, as I was invited to perform for the South Glamorgan schools orchestra at Sophia Gardens Pavilion, a large concert arena near the site of the current SWALEC Stadium, home of Glamorgan County Cricket Club.

The pavilion had staged boxing and wrestling competitions during the 1958 British Empire and Commonwealth Games and also played host to many notable performers in its time, such as Slade, Cliff Richard, Jimi Hendrix, Pink Floyd .... and now Jonathan Power.

I should confess here that my musical abilities were somewhat limited. Incapable of reading music, I simply played along in rough synchronisation with my fellow musicians and turned the pages of my sheet music whenever I saw the others doing it! This was not to be the only time I ducked and dived to make progress in the entertainment world as you will later read.

The performing arts inspired me more than the chalk and talk of the classroom, and I reached the pinnacle of my success when invited by our music teacher Mr Kelly to play the lead role in the school's ambitious production of *Oliver*, based on the novel of Charles Dickens of course. I was the new Mark Lester!

I was revelling in this new-found fame and, as adolescence beckoned, began to observe that my young celebrity status certainly did not harm my luck with the ladies. All in all, it certainly proved a wonderful taster for the fame and fortune I was to experience later in life.

My education continued at nearby Howardian High School; a secondary school first established in Cardiff in 1885. A succession of organisational changes had seen the creation of separate schools for boys and girls but in 1970, the two institutions merged to form Howardian High School.

Sport continued as my main passion in life though, be it football, cricket, or rugby. I was gifted enough to represent the school at all three, though a broken arm sustained whilst playing rugby made a significant dent in my studies, leaving me off school for several weeks and struggling to catch up. I slipped further down the academic ladder as the years rolled by.

The enforced absence made little impact on my academic achievements though, as I rarely took school lessons very seriously at all, preferring to 'muck about' in class rather than devote energy to schoolwork.

The teaching staff at Howardian eventually gave up completely on my prospects of success in the classroom. I was not one of those pupils earmarked for great things by the careers master either. He had little belief in young Power and was convinced that I would come to nothing. These views were shared by his fellow teaching colleagues, and, at such a young age, I was simply ill-equipped to say anything back to them. 'Careers advice' fell within the portfolio of Mr Brain by the way. An unlikely moniker for the man, I always thought.

Funny, I often think about the lack of enthusiasm shown by that uninspiring careers master if I am sitting at the lights in my Bentley, or whimsically enjoying a cocktail in my Chelsea apartment.

Teens are formative years in so many respects of course and, away from the schoolyard, fate also dealt me another card, this time through a modest gift received from a neighbour. It was an autograph book, complete with several well-known signatures. Our neighbour was friends with the late Gil Reece, a Welsh international footballer who eventually made over 300 appearances for Cardiff City, Sheffield United and others.

I set about collecting autographs with vigour and bought a replacement when the first book was full. I collected more and more signatures. I would visit Cardiff City FC, Glamorgan County Cricket Club, and the home of Cardiff Rugby Club, at the famous Cardiff Arms Park, a site now close to the Principality Stadium, in my quest for autographs. I would also hang around the stage door of venues like the New Theatre, Cardiff, hoping for a scribble from a star.

It was a hobby I really enjoyed. As well as collecting the names of course, I especially enjoyed meeting the stars of stage, screen, and sports that I encountered. Little did I perceive then that this teenage boy would one day become integrally involved with the celebrity world and earn a decent crust from it.

As my school days ended, my father once again played a part in my destiny by securing me a position with.... the GPO. I lost even more interest in academic pursuits as a result, safe in the knowledge that the GPO postal services would doubtless deliver me a successful career. Surely, I wouldn't need qualifications to distribute telegrams?

I left school on Friday and started work the following Monday.

I was now a GPO Telegram Boy!

Despite my pride in holding such a lofty title, all was not quite as I had anticipated. Being of no great stature, my oversized GPO uniform made me look, frankly, ridiculous.

As a 16-year-old ready to face the world though, the first challenge I faced was, making tea for the boss.

I was a GPO tea boy, it seems.

I made a lot of tea for bosses back then as I recall, before finally being let loose as a telegram boy, which I soon discovered to be about one rung down the food chain from a postman.

It isn't easy to readily explain the significance of the telegram to the modern world. In the 2020s, your mobile phone can be used to send a picture to Australia, book a holiday or insult the President of the United States. Chances are he might even reply. Communication in 1980 was something else entirely.

Large sections of the public had limited access to a telephone, so telegrams were the only way to send urgent messages across the country quickly. As attendance at events was also often difficult, the sending of a typed note was not uncommon to convey news or extend greetings at events such as weddings. Telegram boys would – in my case – cycle, around the city, delivering these important pieces of text. I was the original iPhone!

Circumnavigating my way around the streets of Cardiff on a Post Office bicycle in all weathers did not make for an easy life. It did, though, bring in a wage. I shall never forget that sensation of my first wage packet. I had arrived in the adult world!

Inevitably I began to date girls, for now, I was armed with newfound wealth from all that pedalling. I dated a local girl, Michelle, for two years. Being older than I was, Michelle also had the added advantage of being able to be served in pubs! Such things are important to a guy at 16.

We both shared a passion for music. We were very avant-garde for the time. Bowie, Roxy Music, and even Kraftwerk, the German electronic band who seemed to hail from another world. We paddled in the waters of punk and splashed about in the New Wave. Paradise Garage catered for our more 'Vivian Westwood' fashion moments while the super cool Hudson & Hudson supplied our high street outfits. Black and white were very in. I thought little of blowing a whole month's salary on just one suit. 1981 was "our year."

Back in the 80s, Michelle and I became swept up by the new romantic Bands like OMD, Culture Club, and Spandau Ballet who held centre stage as, to 'cut a long story short', we swished our way around the Cardiff club scene. Soft Cell would be next on our playlist no doubt. Highlighted hair was of course, compulsory, even for a Telegram Boy.

I also still managed my occasional brushes with celebrities. One memorable highlight occurred when I was tasked with delivering a telegram to Hazel O'Connor by my tea-drinking seniors. She was a notable star in the early 80s and I had been lucky enough to obtain tickets to her concert at the Top Rank. I was a big fan. The prospect of meeting her excited me greatly, even if she would have to witness my ill-fitting GPO uniform.

On arrival at the venue though, I was told that she was unavailable but that the support band would pass on any messages. They had also received a few telegrams, which were gratefully accepted.

This support band delivered an impressive performance during their warmup and practice session, almost outshining Hazel herself later that evening during the actual gig. This bunch of lads from Birmingham sounded superb as they delivered their short set. I followed their career closely over the years. Yes, Duran Duran left a lasting impression on me that night.

Back at work, I enjoyed or maybe endured, a spell as an indoor messenger boy, sorting messages and boiling a kettle. It was all part of the training I suppose as I learned the dull rudiments of my trade.

At 17 years old, the GPO decided I could lose the trusty, rusty bicycle and even graduate from the moped which sometimes carried me and my messages around the city. Courtesy of GPO-sponsored driving lessons, my telegrams were now transported from a minivan. No longer would I negotiate the winds and wetness, exposed to the worst of the Welsh weather. I was the bee's knees in my tiny van, even if I did still have to make the tea.

My 18th birthday saw my elevation to the dizzy heights of Postman, which also included the chance of lucrative shift work. My days as a Telegram Boy were behind me now. The GPO hierarchy would have to find a new office junior to make the tea.

It wasn't quite the golden opportunity I had sought though. That old joke about a career as a postman being better than walking the streets has never made me chuckle. Anyone who smirks along with it has clearly never dragged a wet, heavy mailbag through the streets, trapping their fingers in stiff letter boxes and evading random dogs at every opportunity.

Had we really left the warm, sandy pastures of Pembrokeshire for this? I began to question my father's career choice for his youngest heir. Shift work, especially the night shift, was not compatible with the clubbing lifestyle of a new romantic.

The job was no fun whatsoever. My days of mucking about in the classrooms of Albany Road and Howardian had left me without any qualifications to help pull me out of the corner I had painted myself into. My low pay pointed to no obvious career pathway or promotion prospects ahead. I left the GPO when it split with British Telecoms (BT). I took a position with BT in the post room, where I had previously served time as a young postal trainee. With the unglamorous job title of General Assistant, my lowly wages matched those of the cleaning staff. Disillusioned, the future seemed bleak.

Even my footballing talents seemed to desert me around those times. British Telecommunications adopted a small cartoon yellow bird back then as its logo. 'Buzby' would sit on the animated phone lines issuing merry quips to an increasingly commercialised world. Someone hit on the bright idea of creating a local football team around this feathered friend. 'Buzby's XI' turned out in the Cardiff Civil Service and Commerce League each Sunday morning on the vast, blowy playing fields at Ely, Cardiff. Think Hackney Marshes with a Cardiff accent and you get the general idea.

Now, I didn't consider myself a bad player but, like my fellow Buzbies, all talent seemed to desert me as I pulled on that bright golden jersey. The Busby logo sat proudly on our chests, making us something of a laughing stock for the tough teams who ran amok with us each week. I ponied about in midfield while my co-writer David Collins played full back. He was a plucky enough competitor (imagine the 80s Wales and Liverpool defender Joey Jones but without the pace) though he also fell victim to the curse of Buzby.

We look back and laugh now but these were embarrassing ways to spend Sunday mornings I can tell you. If there was a clash of colours, no other team would ever agree to swap shirts with us as double-figure defeats became the norm. We lost one game 16-1. Our solitary goal may have had a hint of offside about it and the opposition painfully asked, "What about the offside, ref?" The sympathetic official looked back apologetically with a heavy heart. "I know, I know," he sighed. The goal stood.

To haul me away from my miserable BT life, I approached a few London-based drama schools. I had always fancied myself as

24

a bit of an actor since my days alongside the Artful Dodger back at Albany Road.

I received the odd prospectus back and spent time studying *The Stage* newspaper during spells of taking the mail around various BT departments, under the firm but the fair hand of dear old Jill Fleeson.

My enquiries with the London acting establishments taught me two very quick and obvious lessons. Firstly, you had to have the talent. I reckoned I could make a fist of things on that score.

The second criteria would be harder to swing though, as it became clear that some degree of financial influence was also required to pay my way through an acting apprenticeship. The lower ranks of the BT pay scales didn't really leave much scope for that kind of indulgent behaviour I'm afraid.

Jill must have taken pity on her heavy-fringed young mail carrier though, and pointed me to a drama group that existed within BT itself.

'Telstars' were an amateur group that had achieved some success on a UK-wide basis, even performing in Florida. That sounded much more like it I thought. The Florida Hillbillies could work.

Jill persuaded me to audition for a part in a new play being taken on by the group and, following an audition, I was offered a part in their forthcoming production *Eat your Heart Out.*

Eat your heart out indeed, Mr Brain. Careers master.

The rest of the cast all seemed to come from the very senior management grades within BT and the Post Office though they took the young office kid under their collective wing with grace and humility. For the first time in my adult life, I literally shared the stage as an equal. My peers saw no reason why my lowly grade should influence their acceptance of me whatsoever. There was nothing of the 'us and them' shop floor attitudes and I became a valued member of the team.

'Telstars' were a true team and I loved my time with them. We had fantastic times performing at decent venues such as Theatr Clwyd, in North Wales and achieving national recognition.

More importantly, though, it inspired my self-belief that I could hold my own in the company of others, even across our diverse social and economic backgrounds.

In the workplace though, things remained stagnant and uninspiring for me. I moved from the post room to the print room although I was still very much the tea boy/office junior, photocopying and filing endless documents rather than distributing posts. It was an unfulfilling role with few prospects, a fact about which members of the junior management team often reminded me. I was trapped in a non-existent existence and neither valued nor rated by my superiors.

I really wanted more from life than this as I moved through my early twenties. Here I was, in a job with no prospects, still living at home with my parents, shuffling between relationships with a clutch of local girls. The only high spots were the foreign holiday trips to the likes of Ibiza or Majorca, where ambitions ran no higher than enjoying the company of as many girls as possible or drinking until the small hours. Sometimes both.

On one of these beano's, I encountered a lovely girl from Northern Ireland. Kathryn Mackay and I spent most of that holiday in 1984 together. I really missed her when I returned to Wales, and knew that she meant more to me than any other girl I had met to date.

I had fallen in love for the first time.

Kathy was studying at Queen's University, Belfast (often abbreviated to QUB), at the time. Her time was split equally between her parents in Templepatrick and her shared student house in Belfast.

The force of our romance was so strong, as we spent many hours on the telephone and visited each other at every opportunity. My family thought the world of Kathy, as did all my friends. I was prepared to move across to Northern Ireland, such was the strength of my love for her. The relationship though caused some unrest with her parents.

Kathy had experienced a quite different upbringing to me.

Her mother held a senior teaching post while her dad, Dr Mackay, was a senior psychologist. Not a postman in sight.

I approached one of my fellow Telstar troubadours for advice and some help. Ken Spurlock was very senior and enjoyed a regional role. Could he sanction a move for me perhaps? Say, to Belfast? Whilst Ken confirmed that he could help, he had fears for my safety and would not, therefore, sanction the move.

The Northern Ireland 'troubles' were at their height. Catholics and Protestants waged a bloody war of atrocities that stretched back into history. The 80s saw hunger strikes, high-profile killings, and the IRA's bombing of the Grand Hotel in Brighton, which almost wiped out Margaret Thatcher's entire UK Tory government. Ken feared for my safety in such troubled times, even though my experience of such matters extended little beyond the odd U2 track and the Undertones' anthem "Teenage Kicks".

There was also growing resistance to the relationship from across the Irish Sea. Kathy's disapproving parents threatened to pull the plug on her education funding if things weren't halted soon. Kathy was under real pressure to end the relationship, a prospect that left me distraught.

We spoke on the telephone, and I feared the worst. The relationship was struggling. There were tears from Kathy.

I always observed a distinct class difference when I visited her Northern Ireland home and felt socially somewhat out of my depth around her parents. My working-class upbringing in rented accommodation was in sharp contrast to the world created by the occupations of Kathy's parents.

The cards were beginning to stack against me, as I missed a flight to Belfast from Heathrow. My credit card was creaking under the weight of debt arising from sustaining a long-distance relationship. Cash was not in abundance in the pockets of my 80s chinos.

It was time for desperate measures now. Phoning in sick to work, I returned to Heathrow and headed for Belfast. My startled sweetheart collected me from the airport.

After a spot of dutch courage, we headed for 'Chez Kathy'.

Mrs Mc. did not, it is fair to say, share her daughter's delight at seeing the visitor from Wales. "Fuming" does not even come close. In her eyes, I was not welcome on the Emerald Isle, to be sure.

From the kitchen, the sound of Kathy and her mother arguing filled the house. Mother's Scottish tones left her student daughter in no doubt as to which side her bread would be buttered if the relationship continued. I had "no prospects," she ruled. "He will never be capable of looking after you Kathy." "He will achieve nothing."

I stood helplessly in an adjoining room, weary from so many blows.

The contest ended. Kathy threw in the towel on the battered and broken-heartened challenger. It was a victory for Mackay senior. TKO.

On the flight home, I contemplated my future. This wouldn't take long, I observed. My prospects were set out on a single blank page. My 'not to be' mother-in-law had joined a growing list of commentators who had seen little in me. Careers masters, teachers, GPO management. Even those who supported me like Mr Spurlock, felt some of my life choices to be less than sound. Could they all be right? Would their rebuffs and putdowns just become another diary entry? We flew over the rough sea waters.

This can't go on, I thought.

**

The desire to prove these observers wrong overtook me, forming a real turning point in my life. The doubters would be proved wrong, I promised myself.

But how?

As I began to set about a plan to improve my prospects, I took advantage of my well-connected Telstar colleagues. They had shown faith in me but, importantly, also accepted me on a personal level. They looked beyond the Tea Boy. Convinced that I could use my talents on a bigger stage, I was equally convinced that life in the post room or print room was not for me. Promotion was not on the cards given the little confidence or encouragement shown by superiors. It was time for a complete change of career.

The newspaper's small ads began to occupy my attention. This was many years before job seekers would trawl websites for opportunities. The now-defunct *Today* newspaper (1986-1995) often described how one insurance company was constantly on the lookout for consultants. They seemed to feature this advertisement daily for several years. Eventually, I took the bait.

Insurance? What was that?

Churchill Associates would be hearing from me though. After completing the job application, the break I needed came in the form of an invitation to attend an interview in London.

London? Move over Whittington, J Power was coming!

The interview inspired me. A brave new world. The 80s needed bright young talent like mine. The vibrant London office environment scene seemed a lifetime away from my days shifting telegrams and pouring tea. A lifestyle away, even.

Mum and Dad's ambitious plans for the family were rising within me. A resurgent force.

I was appointed as an insurance consultant. Leaving the impressive office, I sucked in the London air. I would prove the doubters wrong; seize the day and grab the opportunity I had created. Hard work would be no discouragement. A new beginning.

To the doubters and detractors, up yours, I thought. My day WILL come.

London Calling

1988 saw me finally leave the dusty corridors of BT to join Churchill Associates.

This was to prove a pivotal moment as my life finally seemed to have clicked into place, almost overnight. The bright lights beckoned. I was ready to meet the challenge.

After successfully navigating the recruitment and selection process, Churchill offered me the post of Financial Consultant. Churchill was an appointed representative of the FTSE 100 company Legal & General (the largest 100 qualifying UK companies by full market value), a household name in the insurance world.

JP was getting somewhere at last.

My first task though, on entering this brave new world, was to buy a suit! The 'baggy jeans and t-shirt look' of my days in the print room would not cut the mustard on the floor of the London Stock Exchange, where I convinced myself that I was surely heading.

A swish suit – the best that high street giant Burtons could offer (not to mention all that I could afford!) – a new shirt, and tie were the order of the day for this bright young upstart. A new, pristine environment awaited. I would not have been out of place on the cover of a David Bowie album in this gear I thought. A briefcase was, of course, a compulsory fashion accessory.

This was the 80s after all.

That first day was to prove an unforgettable experience.

Churchill accommodated me in a hotel near their London base. I must admit, the modest North London location was not quite the 'bright lights' of the big city of which I had dreamed, but all dreams must begin somewhere. "You got to have a dream.... or how are you gonna make a dream come true"? Captain Sensible certainly seemed like a decent judge at the time.

So, proudly, if a little nervously, I took my first steps towards a new life. My first steps to a future that, as time unfolded, would astound me.

A future, that many felt to be beyond even my own wildest dreams.

If they could see me now, that little gang of mine.

At ground zero on that watershed day, my 80s briefcase was empty and bare. Before long though, it became filled with training literature as my new career exploded all around me. "Welcome to the Big Wide World." London Calling. At the Top of the Dial.

I was ready to meet the challenge.

These early steps seem rather mundane now I suppose. 'Skinny Youngster Attends Week-long Training Course.' Hardly makes me out as the 'next big thing', does it?

Many young hopefuls, of varying degrees of ambition, intellect, and ability, probably start out like this. Training and Induction. Icebreaker games on day 1 to ease the nerves. "Think of an alliterative name to describe yourself." (I was always "Powerful Power.") You may have done it yourself.... and probably thought little of it.

To me though, it became life itself. London fired me in the way I had always imagined. New colleagues, senior management. Eager, zealous types. The whole environment had a buzz to it far removed from my earlier life. This was the world for which I had craved. People to whom I could aspire. Energetic, ambitious, hungry, and driven. Follow that dream, boy.

The first week passed in the blink of an eye.

The intensive induction course covered the very basics of financial services, customs, rules, regulations, procedures, and basic products. Doesn't sound much, does it?

Read on....

Come to the end of the week, I was duly accredited, licensed, and signed off to advise clients on matters such as life assurance, savings, products, and pensions. "Your life in my hands," I mused quietly to myself. The tie still sat neatly in place, despite a demanding and intense induction program. Windsor knot, by the way.

31

I kid ye knot.

Further training was to follow but I was let loose on the market.

Setting off like an express train I began selling products and packages to all and sundry. Old acquaintances, new clients. They all felt the force of Powerful Power as I embraced my new world with gusto. Work hard; work smart, they urged. I did not need to be told twice.

Churchill instigated an innovative marketing strategy in collaboration with a holiday company. This featured the offer of a week's holiday to any customer who signed up to one of our policies. These were the days of the timeshare holiday and any new customer who, having purchased a product, went on to recommend us to two new clients benefitted from a free overseas trip – provided the two new guys signed up as well of course.

It is all a bit of a distant memory now I'm afraid, and I am sure that many clients were more attracted by the appeal of a free junket abroad than the delights of life assurance but hey, all business is good business, as I was quickly coming to realise. Referrals and recommendations came thick and fast. This was the "Modern World" in which Paul Weller had sung.

My day would start early. I became very organised. I simply had to be as, for the first time ever, I was now working alone. I had to generate my own business leads and organise client meetings. These were long days, and the evenings were filled with visiting clients, advising them on all aspects of financial services. I revelled in all this though, as I would have worked 24 hours a day, 7 days a week if I could.

Powerful Power's enthusiasm, drive, and success soon came to the attention of the top brass. They summoned me to attend HQ for a dialogue with the company's MD. Positive feedback from the Chief Executive, Colin Hill, had caused some sharp ears to prick up it seemed. We can use this new Welsh voice from the hillsides.

Details of Churchill's ambitious and progressive expansion plans were revealed to me. It seemed that these plans envisaged a centre in Wales.......and did I fancy it?

To describe my reaction as joyous would not come even close to how I felt. Not only was it a chance to "sign for home club" so to speak but, more significantly, the offer represented an overwhelming display of confidence. I had only been with the firm a short time yet here was the MD presenting me with an opportunity to reach the next level. It was a remarkable moment in my young career.

I was ready to talk terms.

The offer would consist of a basic salary, expenses, and commission. I later realised that this was standard fayre for the kind of position on offer, though at the time the whole package felt light years away from my BT experience.

Churchill's decision to invest in me so heavily and back with me hard cash represented a watershed moment in my fledgling career. The level of trust and backing sent my confidence soaring.

My goals would be to secure office accommodation, recruit a team of sales staff, and establish a strong identity for a significant London name miles away in Wales. We were probably looking at central Cardiff, close to my old stomping grounds.

Talk about "no pressure!"

Determined to shirk not one jot from the chance, I seized the moment with both hands.

Seize the day, they say. Seize the day.

My first success saw the acquisition of office accommodation near the centre of the Welsh capital. Just a stone's throw out of town, on Cowbridge Road East, our new home above a hearing aid company was my window to the world. A single room in these modest surroundings meant that I could now meet prospective clients and recruit staff from within my own office accommodation.

It is hard to imagine the boost this gave me though I would later learn important lessons from it.

I was becoming my own man, under the guiding tutelage of the main company. Captain of the team, though with a reassuring arm around my shoulder if needed. In time I came to realise just how much of a safety net that that would become by the way. That's a story for later though.

I grew my team around me. Hand-picked with a sales background.

No salaries.

Remuneration was based 100% on commission. They knew the score. Our roost above Hidden Hearing was no place for the faint-hearted but was home to some hidden talents, all of whom shared that hunger; that drive that Churchill saw in me. "Oh yes." My team.

Churchill continued to back me, providing training opportunities for myself and my team at the 5-star Swallow Hotel on the outskirts of London. A generous expense account ensured that my guys were well looked after. The glitz and trappings of London life were slowly trickling their way down the M4 to Cowbridge Road East.

The brave world exploded all around me, as the excitement and pull of it all drew me further in.

Here's a story for you from those times.

One evening at dinner. London. Hotel accommodation was provided by Churchill. Top of the range, of course.

Quietly, almost unnoticed, an announcement echoed around the luxurious foyer ....

"Would Mr Gascoigne please report to reception?"

My ears pricked up. "It can't be, can it?"

Yes, it was.

It was THAT Mr Gascoigne. Gazza himself.

Seizing the moment again, I ventured to introduce myself. Giving little thought as to how a charismatic character such as himself would react to my direct approach, I extended an introduction to him. What could possibly go wrong?

Many people speak with real affection about Gazza. Lineker, Shearer, Sir Bobby Robson.

Giants of the football world would roll their eyes and smile at the very mention of his name. Mums wept alongside him during

Italia 90. A whole nation loved him.

Let me tell you this affection is richly deserved, for Gazza was simply different class that night. A top man, indeed.

An hour passed in his glittering company. His new club, Tottenham Hotspur was putting him up in the same top hotel that we were using. In effect, we were in Gazza's home….and how welcome he made me.

Forget his offer of match tickets, the luxury surroundings, and London lights - Gazza was simply quality. We talked like old mates who had years to catch up on. The man is 100% pure Geordie Gold. I would meet him many times years down the years and never would I grow weary of his company. Anyway, I digress.

These were heady, yet turbulent times. Life on a commission -only salary is not for everyone. It's life on the edge, the bleeding edge. Some of my team thrived, some…fell on stony ground. Some bloomed, some withered. Ambitions were satisfied as there was simply no ceiling to our potential.

There was no floor either mind.

Sales and earnings could be erratic. Some months would be amazing, others could be a disaster. This was typical of most commission-only direct sales teams back then. It was no place for the faint-hearted, though the rewards were out there for sure.

This was a time of buoyancy and confidence in the economic and political world. Thatcher and Reagan preached to a new brand of 'can-do' private sector, profit-driven disciples. Hard work would be rewarded. By the time I leaped aboard the gravy train the tracks were well laid out. Monetarism rules, ok? Reduce public expenditure and create your own wealth. Keith Joseph wooed Thatcher, who wooed the rest of us. Keep the money supply down then jump aboard and fill in the gaps. There was money to be made…. if you had the balls.

Loadsamoney.

And boy, did I have the balls.

Did I understand the wider impact of Thatcher's macroeconomic policies on working-class communities at the time? Probably not. Were the humble folk of Newcastle, Glasgow, and South Wales disenfranchised by the 80s? Not everyone could buy a ticket for the gravy train and, looking back on it now, I see the impact of the Thatcher Years on working class Britain. The industrial unrest, the have and have nots. The disruption of communities.

I was not wholly dazzled by the Tory blue headlights of course. My South Wales upbringing would soon put a stop to that. I did appreciate the impact value of hard work though. I put in the hours. I took the risks. I started a long way back and was prepared to show effort, enterprise, and innovation. These words mean the same in Henley as they do in Haverfordwest.

Hard work and ambition are the same in any language.

My early life seemed a world away. Those sure footings put in place by my parents provided a foundation for success. Dreams don't come easy...but something caught my eye. This was a world for which I craved, as the 80s wrapped themselves around me. "Don't You Want Me, Baby?"

I shared a cool Cardiff Bay apartment with my girlfriend Tracy Osmond. Ambitious, go-getter types occupied the neighbouring apartments in this prestigious, waterside development in the new, beating heart of the Welsh capital.

A barrage kept the River Taff in check, ensuring a land of marinas and eateries where muddy riverbanks had previously carved their way through Tiger Bay. Even the very wind and waves obeyed this new, entrepreneurial drive it seemed.

I was going from strength to strength. And I was not up for stopping.

As my career moved on, my confidence simply grew. I received excellent support from Churchill as I learned quickly on the 'shop floor'.

News of potential changes in the upper echelons of Churchill reached my ears, with talk of new ventures. I avoided the inevitable politics and gossip associated with such speculation. but watched developments quietly from the sidelines. Could this lead to an opening? I was always open to an opening.

Perhaps arising from these whispers in the shadows, an approach was made to me by one of the directors. The offer comprised an attractive package that exceeded my existing terms.

I did not hesitate, and soon joined the ranks of the newly formed Highland Financial Services. The business model was close to that of Churchill, with links to Eagle Star also. Life looked set to continue in the fine form to which I was becoming accustomed.

Calls from clients were soon accompanied by approaches from CEOs and other senior figures, as my head became hunted by the movers and shakers of the financial world. My growing reputation was pricking up some sharp ears indeed.

Our premises in Cowbridge Road East were owned by Mark Moss who had founded Hidden Hearing in 1984. Mark was a man of tremendous drive. Hidden Hearing was eventually floated on the stock market in 1998 and sold to a Danish multinational in 2000 for example. He was always a guy worth listening to.

Mark made a significant career within the world of hearing aids and mobility devices. An entrepreneur of the highest standing. Ultimately, he became a man of considerable wealth. His impressive property portfolio included a beautiful home in Nottage, a village within Porthcawl, a well-known attraction on the South Wales coast just a short drive westwards out of Cardiff. Bungalows, sweeping sands, and a link golf course gaze out across the Bristol Channel here. Beyond the Bristol Channel lies the Atlantic Ocean.

Mark would patiently listen to my ambitious business plans late into the evening. Did he see something of his young self in me? Perhaps. I soaked up his knowledge, experience, and acumen like a sponge, learning from someone whose record of achievement in the business world left many gasping. In exchange, Mark admired my achievement in growing a company within such a short timescale. I learned from him about the importance of taking advantage of opportunities. Echoes of my dear old dad I thought.

To my astonishment, Mark felt that the time had already come for me to consider ploughing my own furrow. I had earned a terrific reputation during my short financial career to date but the real opportunity was there for me now, he observed. What is more, he would provide investment funds to back me if I had the venture drive in me.

Events were unfolding with pace as the world lay in wait for me. Could I make it alone? Could I flourish in the swirling waters of private enterprise, paddling my own canoe? Would I sink or swim?

Or should I continue to work for a third party, working hard to chase the commission-based salary upon which we all relied?

"Mark," I said. "I am in!"

Power Financial Services Ltd. was born.

This really was a whole new world. Mark was supportive but, of course, had his own affairs to manage. No longer was I Branch Manager with the support of others, I now owned the business outright. My name was above the shop.

Assembling a team of hungry staff, engaged on commission - only contracts I threw myself into meeting the needs of my clients. Running a business for the first time, I led the team in supporting new and existing clients, thriving on the buzz of selling our financial products, and motivating the team.

As the principal of PFS, I signed terms, firstly with Eagle Star then later, Legal & General to be our product providers. As well as having a sales team in Cardiff, I also recruited two financial consultants in London, Andrew Macey, and Dwayne Cowans. Dwayne was the brother of England fast bowler Norman Cowans. I met Norman on a few occasions. On one occasion, he gave me a behind-the-scenes tour of Lord's cricket ground. As a huge cricket fan, that was a real thrill and an example of the glamour associated with the work at times.

Much harder to take though, was that feeling of isolation. Being 100% accountable for every aspect of the business, the buck stopped firmly at my door, with no supportive network on hand to meet any training or development needs I faced. No arm around the shoulder now.

I found myself with less time available for the sales side of things as running the new business of Power Financial Services became more of a commitment. All consuming, even.

Staffing, accounts, audit, premises management, corporate governance. These were steep learning curves for the young whizz-kid as I learned on the job, about the pressures, constraints and challenges of establishing, maintaining, and developing a new business venture. Struggling to keep my eye on the ball, I eventually began to have second thoughts.

Had I taken the plunge too early? Should I have spent more time in my water wings before contemplating the unchartered waters of running my own business? A continuing series of telephone calls from competitors etc. told me that my name still had some currency out there. These people were ready to toss me a lifebelt if I felt the need to jump ship. I confess that my head became turned by these potential suitors.

It was time to call on the advice of my mentor, Mark Moss. Feeling distinctively out of my depth, I was no longer able to devote my energy to the sales side of things. Losing my focus, a feeling of vulnerability came upon me. This was a new emotion for a youth hitherto driven by self-belief and confidence.

Mark understood my pain. He knew that my ambition was my power source; but I had to do what was best for me, he advised. It would be my decision.

I held a few tentative discussions with potential business partners who were ready to take me on board if I decided to leave behind the idea of running my own business. There would be no shame in admitting defeat, I told myself. "Better to have loved & lost," so to speak. I had given it a go. I could look at myself in the mirror with a clean conscience.

Eventually, I accepted an offer from Pioneer Mutual for the position of Sales Manager. Power Financial Services was no more. I even sold the company name to the South Wales Electricity Board!

I went on to enjoy my stint at Pioneer. Their remuneration

package rewarded my sales skills handsomely as I threw myself into my new role, building a new team in the way I always enjoyed. The power was returning to my veins.

The company underwent a reorganisation, becoming Swiss Pioneer Life, and was a giant in the financial world, a real powerhouse. All staff was summoned to discuss the future. Was there to be exciting news?

It became clear though that Swiss Life was not inclined to retain a direct sales force. We received the devastating news that our roles were to be terminated. This was a huge blow and I reflected on some of the extremely attractive financial packages I had rejected from other companies before committing myself to Pioneer, only to now discover that my services were no longer required. This was a low I had yet to come across in my career to date.

As if the news of the loss of our jobs wasn't bad enough, I started to receive commission repayment demands from the product providers that had served the now defunct Power Financial Services. It became clear that since the company closed, many customers, via the financial consultants that had once worked with us, had cancelled their policies. Under the terms of the contract that I signed as Principal, any policy that was cancelled within the first couple of years of the policy running would result in a repayment of commission.

If I wasn't previously aware of what "commission reclaim" meant, I certainly was now. The demands were coming thick and fast and amounted to several thousands of pounds, a huge sum of money back then. It came as a massive shock and took me several years to repay. It certainly had a huge effect on my earnings going forward, as each month I had to repay large sums of money out of my income to repay a lingering debt. This was a bitter pill to swallow.

I quickly realised that greater quality control of the business was required. There was little point in having advisors writing loads of business only for large amounts of cancellations to take place. The principal would have to bite the bullet and be responsible for any future debt liability. This taught me a valuable lesson going forward, and one I would implement in my future business planning arrangements.

As the rest of the team considered their options, I became aware of an opportunity with Legal & General Assurance Company. I was aware of the reputation which L&G enjoyed across the financial sector from my experience to date. It seemed a natural fit.

A jump straight into a managerial post would probably not quite be on the cards just yet, but the offer of a position as financial consultant with the prospect of a managerial role if things worked out, sounded like a decent way forward. The career could be back on the up if things worked out.

The new role would see me taken on in a self-employed capacity on a commission-only basis. I took a longer-term view of this opportunity to reignite my career though, looking forward to re-establishing my reputation with a major insurance name.

Throwing myself into the new position with customary vigour, I sold the products offered by Legal & General to a growing customer base. I quickly outperformed my colleagues and soon came to the attention of senior management, receiving regular invitations to the 'Lunch of the Month' receptions at a top Cardiff restaurant for the best-performing advisers. These Friday afternoon & evening sessions were a terrific way to wine and dine in the capital. Other incentives included trips to exotic overseas locations as I took to life eagerly. Even the hangovers seemed fun back then!

Before too long, in recognition of my performance and potential, Area Manager John Mathias sounded me out about a managerial position. John was later to emerge as a pivotal character in my development. His superb managerial skills set me on a path that guided my future career. He realised and nurtured the potential of my networking ability and saw the unique opportunities which could lay ahead for me, working with sports and entertainment clients.

It was the news for which I had been waiting, as I threw

41

myself fully behind L&G. Following a few days of assessment, I joined a cohort of other new managers on extremely lucrative remuneration terms & conditions: a significant salary, company car, expenses, and bonuses. It was the stuff of dreams at last, as I established myself as a leading light within this FTSE 100 company.

Trips to Hong Kong, China, and Mexico stand out as memories from these happy times. I recall one remarkable highlight when the entertainment at our intimate Legal & General Gala Dinner was provided by none other than the Beach Boys! I was certainly picking up the 'good vibrations' as the demanding job with this major financial institution began to reap its reward. I felt secure and content. Further promotion came quickly. Jonathan Power, Executive Sales Manager.

Despite being a time of reward and achievement, these were also times of learning for me. I remember one development especially. It boosted my career back then, drawing on my skills. The learning has stayed with me to this day, guiding my future business decisions and activities.

John Mathias was, once again, at the heart of things. He noticed how well I had combined the role of manager with continuing success in the sales field.

At the time I was good friends with the manager of Cardiff City FC, the late Eddie May.

As a no-nonsense defender with Wrexham in the 70s, Eddie had established a solid reputation in the lower echelons of the football world. He was now making a decent job of running Cardiff City, inspiring my hometown team to a league and cup double success during the days of the old 4th Division (now League 2). Eddie was a well-known figure across the Welsh soccer scene. With 90 appearances for Swansea City as a player and even a short spell with Newport County as a coach, he is one of the few men to be associated with all four of Wales's senior clubs. Eddie would prove a most useful contact down the years before his sad passing in 2012.

It wasn't all figures from the world of sport though as clients also included the colourful BBC Wales presenter Chris Needs at that time. To those outside Wales, Chris is probably best described as "flamboyant." Somewhere between Graham Norton and Terry Wogan perhaps. His regular night-time radio show provided an eclectic mix of music and chat, including many emotional and affectionate phone-ins with members of his Friendly Garden, an informal network of listeners created by the host to provide comfort and company to those in need of such support. The Garden boasted almost 50,000 members, mainly from Wales but even as far away as Australia. For his charity work and services to broadcasting, he was awarded an MBE in 2005 and a Variety Club of Great Britain Lifetime Achievement Award in 2009.

Sadly, dear Chris left us in July 2020.

So, noticing that my clients were beginning to span a broad spectrum of the local sporting and entertainment world, John observed that perhaps I could be onto something here. Was there scope to set up a Business Club, he mused? L&G would provide the backing and support network.

John's idea changed everything for me. It was the start of big things.

Really big things.

The Business Club project would utilise my networking skills and draw upon my ability to forge relationships with high-profile individuals.

John and I were fully behind the idea. I saw the initiative as very much 'my baby.' The business model would see me head up the project, with the task of introducing both myself and Legal & General to a wider community. Connecting people to people. L&G would provide back-office support and fund luncheons etc. The South Wales Young Executive Club was born.

The constitutional arrangements for the new venture prescribed that membership would be provided strictly on an invitation-only basis.

The first gathering saw Eddie May joined by a mutual friend Andrew Costley, a local lawyer, and Falklands hero Simon

Weston. Caerphilly-born Weston had been severely injured aboard the Sir Galahad during the 1982 conflict in the South Atlantic, incurring 46% burns. Despite the trauma, he had gone on to establish himself as a well-known champion of the veterans' cause. He also set up the national youth charity, Weston Spirit, in 1988 with Paul Oginsky and Ben Harrison.

Welsh rugby's Robert Jones was also present along with highly acclaimed local boxing manager Dai Gardner amongst others. Jones alone went on to earn over 50 caps for Wales as a scrum half of some skill. He also turned out for the British & Irish Lions and the Barbarians before enjoying a media career, especially through the medium of Welsh.

We were putting together a decent little lineup for our new venture. International names, world champions, and local legends. As friendships began to develop, we would all look forward to the next meet-up.

Gardner was especially enthusiastic about the project. He was a well-known figure across the boxing scene, having steered South Wales's own Robbie Regan to several world title shots, including success at the WBO level to claim the bantamweight crown in 1996.

His other fighters included the late Johnny Owen – the Merthyr Matchstick. Owen challenged WBC Champion, Lupe Pintor, for the world bantamweight crown in September 1980, losing the fight following a twelfth-round knockout after being floored for the third time. Owen left the ring on a stretcher and never regained consciousness. He fell into a coma and died seven weeks later in a Los Angeles hospital at the age of 24.

Gardner also represented WBO Featherweight Champion, Steve Robinson. Cardiff-born Robinson was an unlikely yet worthy champion with seven successful defences of his title, before eventually falling to Sheffield's Prince Naseem Hamed in 1995.

Gardner was keen to establish an organisation to which he could refer his boxers and trainers for financial advice. Eddie May also began to refer Cardiff City players toward us as the Young Executive Club gathered pace.

It soon became clear that any aspiring sports personality or entertainment figure in South Wales would be well advised to seek out the services of myself at Legal & General as my reputation grew. My client list developed as word spread. I believed that I had found my niche as, although still performing with success as a manager, I began to emerge as the 'go-to' person for advice and support to stars of the local sporting and entertainment scene. I began to realise that this was where I wanted to position myself going forward.

These were fun times as you might appreciate. Chris Needs was always plugging us on his late-night radio shows and our office staff inevitably bristled with excitement as a growing list of famous names continued to pop along to our offices. Even the former autograph-hunting manager used to enjoy these visits!

Many top names became my personal friends. Steve Robinson and I would holiday abroad together with our girlfriends for example. FIFA registered referee Howard King also became a friend.

Howard was a great character who I even tried to persuade to join us at Legal & General as he was due to leave his position as a commercial manager down the road at Ninian Park, the home of Cardiff City FC.

As a City fan at heart still, I was also delighted to be able to support the club through sponsorship arrangements and advertisements in the match programmes. It wasn't all 'stars in their eyes' stuff mind, as I knew that this was all good exposure for us, helping to establish our brand across a wider customer base.

Howard would tell some great stories from his days in the upper tiers of the football world. My favourite probably concerned the time he blew for full-time early in a fixture involving Manchester United because he was due to return to a party in his hometown of Merthyr Tydfil that evening! Alex Fergusson's reaction is probably best not repeated in these pages. Perhaps that was when the concept of Fergie Time was first invented. Great times. Great memories.

Other stories were less colourful though. Despite a long career officiating at some top games across Europe, Howard's financial position was not strong. He hoped that releasing his memoirs might ease his burden. He wondered if I might be able to broker a deal through a contact I had at the *News of the World* newspaper.

I was happy to help Howard in any way I could, but it was important that he understood what he was letting himself in for. His story was most likely to attract international attention with the distinct possibility of some impact on his reputation.

Howard decided to go ahead though and yes, the story caught the imagination of the tabloid media. Tales emerged of his acceptance of offers to enjoy the complimentary company of beautiful ladies whilst in charge of matches on the continent. I am not sure how much Howard enjoyed the exposure, though he was paid for his contribution by the newspaper. I declined a fee.

Other colourful developments emerged. One client sought my support to help stage a boy band concert in the nearby town of Barry – a town later to find national fame thanks to the hit TV show Gavin & Stacey. I was to be a music producer! We went the whole hog. We arranged a venue, set a date, and even sold tickets. Excitement grew, though the young Irish band was relatively unknown at the time.

Unfortunately, show business does not always go to plan and we learned at the 11th hour that the band could not fulfil the engagement. There was no alternative but to refund the ticket money and cancel the gig. It is anyone's guess what that night may have led to, as the hitherto unknown Boyzone went on to achieve high stardom. Shame they missed out on that Barry gig though eh?

***

Cancelled gigs with would-be aspiring pop performers aside, I must confess that things were going well. The 'Power Star' was most definitely in the ascendancy.

My new career saw me supporting and socialising with a host of well-known names. I also held down a challenging role as a high-profile manager with a recognised insurance company. Yes, things could have been worse I suppose.

But doubt was beginning to form though in the dark recesses of my mind. It began slowly but gathered pace as my career blossomed.

I always felt that I acted with integrity, offering advice to my growing client base on the best products that Legal & General could offer.

That was just it though. I was, inevitably, tied into the L&G products. I could only offer the services of the firm for whom I worked. They paid my wages after all.

Unable to promote the services of other companies though, I just couldn't help but contemplate a future whereby I might one day offer advice across a wider portfolio of products and services. Whilst Legal & General was a superb company, they were not number one when it came to every category of financial services. No single company could be of course.

Clients came to me for advice. Many were not comfortable in the complex world of insurance, life assurance, pension policies, and such. That was my job. They needed impartial, honest advice from somebody who could demystify this complex world. Could I really do that if I was only offering products from one supplier? It would be like telling someone they should only shop in Tesco when you knew that perhaps Asda or Waitrose also had some good deals available.

It began to niggle me. Deep down, I knew that my clients required impartial, independent advice.

The key word here is 'independent.' The advice would not be restricted to the services or products of a single company. Knowledge of the broader financial services landscape would bring a much wider benefit to clients than I could at the time. They would be free from the constraints of the one-stop shop. The concept appealed to me.

Suddenly, I was faced with a decision. Legal & General

rewarded my efforts with generous terms & conditions. Frankly, I was not short of a bob or two, thank you very much. The job security provided by a FTSE 100 listed company also counted for a great deal. I benefited from the absolute best management training and the wise counsel of gurus such as John Mathias, Basil Dodd, Tony Weaver, and Scott Howells. I led a terrific team and enjoyed the rich trappings of success.

But…

In my heart of hearts, I knew that a new door lay in wait. I knew that I was right in my ideas. If I was to truly earn the respect of my clients, then surely, I must point them to the best advice available, not simply the best that Legal & General could deliver. The client base established through my hard work in developing the potential of the South Wales Young Executive Club had brought me a clientele that was simply on another level to my contemporaries. I had to maximise the benefits available to them.

Around this time, Regional Director Tony Weaver departed Legal & General to set up Heartland Independent Financial Advisers. Several of his former colleagues followed. The call to me soon came.

Tony had overseen my successful contribution to Legal & General. He had ultimately been responsible for overseeing my various promotions. More significantly though, Tony had noted the type of clients I was attracting and advising. If I was to succeed further, he felt that I should make the move to join his national network of independent financial advisers.

In truth, this dilemma had occupied my mind increasingly for some time. I had become distracted by it. Consumed even, as I began to take my eye off the ball. It would be a massive decision. I weighed up my options. A generous remuneration package within an established company versus a commission-only contract based purely upon the business I could generate. How many would contemplate such a risk?

It was a watershed moment. Do I stick or twist? Would I stay in the waters I knew or set course for a new world? A world where riches could be made and, just as importantly, a lifelong business reputation for integrity, honesty, and care for the client could be established, developed, and maintained.

Deal or No Deal?

Although I certainly thought long and hard about this important decision, I suspect that I knew the course I would take.

I decided that the time had been reached to end my association with Legal & General and face a new challenge. Leaving behind the safety net and security that L&G offered, I decided to throw in my lot as an independent financial adviser with Heartland Independent Advisers.

I was ready to open the box.

The fledgling company was still in its infancy. I was offered a deal that comprised a 70/30 split in terms of commission/fee income, the same terms as all new advisers would attract. Each adviser would retain 70% of commission income with the remaining 30% going to the company. We would be provided with the services of a desk, telephone, basic administrative support, and a full Quality Control (compliance) service which would ensure that the advice we offered really was the best advice. Home would be an office based in Windsor Place in the heart of Cardiff City Centre. The set-up there perhaps resembled that of a barrister's chambers.

Notwithstanding the support available, each adviser operated on a solely self-employed basis with responsibility for business generation.

The option to provide advice across a range of products filled me with excitement. I could finally offer truly independent advice across the whole spectrum of financial services. I knew just how much my clients would benefit from this.

In addition to the 30% that I paid to Heartland, I also handed over an additional 10% to an in-house research assistant who would conduct a full company and sector-wide product check based on the advice that was required. This important background work was fundamental in helping me to deliver the best advice to my client.

The backing I received from my existing clientele was a

source of great encouragement to me at the time. Each one of them stuck with me, recognising the advantages which could accrue from my access to a wider knowledge base.

In addition to ploughing my own furrow within this new environment, I also found myself free of the responsibilities of team management.

Whilst this had been an aspect of my earlier roles that I enjoyed; the newfound freedom allowed me to commit myself fully to serving my clients in a new, uninhibited way. I quickly familiarised myself with new products and procedures and soon built up a significant amount of business as I developed my own business model.

My phone never stopped ringing as I developed and maintained the reputation I sought, namely a source of impartial, credible advice to both new and existing clients from the worlds of sport and entertainment. The decision paid off handsomely as referrals and new clients came thick and fast.

By way of illustration, I recall, for example, how one client, former England goalkeeper David James, once asked to call up Arsenal legend Ian Wright.

I gave Ian Wright a call but my first meeting with Ian and his wife Debbie did not go well. This was before the days of Sat Nav, and finding his house proved a real hurdle. Fortunately, I managed to seek directions as I filled up for fuel, racing off then into the night to arrive at 'Chez Wrighty', where I paused to ring my host.

To my horror though, I discovered that I had left my wallet back at the petrol station.

Unsurprisingly, there was no sign of the wallet back at the station and I returned to my potential new clients in something of a state. What would they think of this bedraggled, confused Welshman who couldn't follow simple directions or even look after simple possessions? The first hour of that first encounter consisted of a series of phone calls from me trying to cancel credit cards etc.

Anyway, Ian and Debbie became clients of mine, despite the

clumsiness of these opening exchanges. Debbie's experience in the banking and financial sector was invaluable on that first evening. She had worked for a major, high-street bank and her grasp of financial issues was a great help. Perhaps they just took pity on me that night or maybe they recognised the genuine guy in front of them. It came as a great thrill later to be invited to a special party thrown by Debbie to celebrate Ian breaking the Arsenal goalscoring record.

It was also a real pleasure to attend one of his TV chat shows with Joe Calzaghe as my guest. We mingled in the green room with someone called Tom Jones and a certain Lennox Lewis. For two boxing fans from Wales, it was quite a night!

These little stories just give you a flavour of the sort of clients I had and the connections that were made.

My client list read like a 'who's who' of the sporting scene, Premiership footballers, international rugby stars, and world champions from the boxing ring. Even the agents of top players began to refer their own clients to me for advice.

These were heady times indeed, although I could feel that, in some ways, my success was counting against me. The 30% of the income which I was required to contribute to the company far exceeded the amount raised by my contemporaries in sheer monetary terms. Was this fair I wondered?

In terms of actual cash, 30% represented a significant contribution from me, though the admin support, etc. which I received was broadly on a par with that provided to my fellow advisers in the Cardiff office. 30% of my takings far exceeded 30% earned by some of the others I can tell you. I also had to find the funds for the additional secretarial and research backup to support the considerable volume of business I was generating. That all came out of the remaining 70% by the way.

The monthly 'league tables' which showed the performance of each adviser served only to underpin the resentment and jealousy which some felt. The figures strengthened my feeling that I was paying over the odds here.

I also resented the 'autograph hunting' undertaken by my

colleagues whenever my famous clients attended our offices. This was simply unprofessional, and I took no time in making my feelings known on the matter. Stars are always happy to scribble in a fan's notebook, as I knew from my adolescence but there is a time and a place, you know.

Amazingly, some of the other advisers even began to mailshot footballers at random, offering advice. The first time I became aware of this happening was when one of my own clients rang me, having received such a notification.

This situation was farcical and bordered on insulting. Poaching from a colleague. Really?

I had been happy at Heartland overall, but the writing was on the wall now.

After a short consultation with senior management, I let it be known that I would be terminating my arrangement with Heartland Independent Advisers. Notwithstanding my disgust at some of the above goings on, I knew that I had already outgrown the place.

I was ready to go it alone once more, though this time I was confident and experienced. I knew that there was a vibrant market out there for me. A world was ready out there. I knew that I had the guts and application to make a go of it. It was 1999 and Jonathan Power Associates Ltd. was ready to hit the streets.

New office accommodation became available at the site of the World Trade Centre in the city centre. I managed to negotiate terms with Interlink Premier Network, a similar type of organisation to Heartland, based in Wales though, this time on a 93/7% split. This included the full compliance service that I sought. All work was fully vetted and signed off by external compliance officers.

True to form, my clients remained loyal. The long hours required to make JPA a success represented no barrier to me, as my business became my hobby, and my hobby became my business. The business called for my full attention, and I threw myself into it with gusto, focused on making a success of it.

I operated with a small, tight, team. I was supported by two support staff and two independent financial advisers. This model became a feature of the way I would come to operate down the years.

It was to prove a very lucrative hobby, trust me. My earnings brought me a luxury house in a desirable area of Cardiff and a top-of-the-range sports car. My parents would want for nothing as I laid the foundations for a comfortable old age. As I have said before in these pages, if you have the ambition, matched with drive, hard work, and a degree of acumen or ability, these things can be within your reach. It had been a bumpy ride to the top, but the view was worth it.

International household names featured in my phone book as the sky really became the limit. It was a great life, though our hard work in establishing such a high-profile client base had not gone unnoticed.

Financial institutions were desperate to do business with us. Corporate hospitality packages were offered to me as invitations to major sporting events became the norm, such was the level at which we were operating and the extent to which we were courted by the market. A box at the *Last Night of the Proms* stands out as one memorable highlight for example. The Woolwich Building Society even designed a special mortgage product exclusively for our clients. This unique, fixed-rate policy was the cheapest on the market at the time. £10 million of lending was set aside for the project. The full amount was taken up in a heartbeat as clients clamoured to come on board. More pressure on my already exhausted phone.

The breadth of products we were able to offer was so important. Bespoke packages designed by major insurance outfits exclusively for our clients sat alongside existing products offered by a range of brokers with whom we forged links. Buildings & contents insurance, car insurance, and career-ending injury cover. A smorgasbord of products to lay before our hungry clients.

Former footballers such as Tottenham and England's Gary Stevens and Ian Wright linked up with us in relation to career - ending injury cover. Wrighty was in partnership with well-known businesswoman Melanie Burns.

In collaboration with London-based Prager & Fenton Accountancy firm, we also devised a 'free' accountancy service for elite clients. I would pay the accountancy fees instead of my clients. It was a bit of a loss leader but a tremendous incentive to my clients. We were developing into a 'one-stop shop' for a client base who snapped up the expertise that we were able to steer their way. This kind of service was tailor-made for the fast-paced world of the professional athlete, where fortunes could be put at risk by a single late tackle. Word of our services spread, as we gained a firm foothold in the elite market.

As an independent financial advice firm with access to legal and accountancy advice, we were able to provide our clients with a comprehensive support package. This was a significant improvement on the restricted assistance I could provide from within Legal & General.

Prager & Fenton accountants soon saw the advantages of our setup and began to refer clients our way for independent financial advice suited to elite-level clients from the entertainment world, including rock legend Greg Lake and Soul II Soul star Caron Wheeler as our reputation grew. The addition of Sir Geoff Hurst to our ranks as Non-Executive Director added further to our credibility. More of Sir Geoff later.

After one year of trading, I knew that I had made the right decision. We had established our name within a niche market.

As our name began to become well-known, I was approached by the agent of international goalkeeping star David James, Colin Gordon, who wanted to see if I would meet with finance company Kingsbridge PLC, which also specialised in the world of sport and entertainment.

Kingsbridge was an established operator in the field, and I was very much the new kid on the block, though they had become aware of my company and I. They were keen to meet, following their recent flotation on the stock market.

I was lukewarm about any proposed collaboration as I was very protective of my business and clientele. I decided to go ahead though with a meeting. Curiosity as much as anything else may have been behind that decision.

At the very cordial meeting which ensued, it became clear that these guys had done their homework. They knew that my clients included Joe Calzaghe, Steve Robinson, Craig Bellamy, Wrighty, Dutch soccer star Nordin Wooter and England rugby internationals Victor Ubogo and Mike Catt. Our growing client base also included a host of pop stars and songwriters alongside a sprinkling of high net-worth clients from the worlds of medicine, law, and finance.

Kingsbridge's expansion had led to their acquisition of firms in Scotland, London, and the Midlands. We were well placed for them geographically. Things were left on the basis that Kingsbridge would discuss the matter at board level and return to me. I put it to the back of my mind and resumed 'business as usual.'

It soon became clear that it had not gone to the back of Kingsbridge's mind though. Far from it, judging by the increasing number of calls I received from them as they outlined their proposal to buy me out, and add myself and my company to their existing business portfolio. We had only been in operation for a single year yet here was now a stock market listed company with genuine plans to take us over.

Whilst keeping my cards close to my chest, I was nevertheless obliged to give the proposal serious thought. I decided to seek the wise counsel of Mark Boomla, senior partner at Prager & Fenton. Mark was a "no-nonsense" kind of guy who I knew would offer constructive and measured food for thought. Mark saw little harm in at least providing Kingsbridge with the necessary information which they would require to make a proper offer. There would be no harm in seeing what was on the table was there?

Mark agreed to act as my corporate adviser and oversee the process. The appropriate governance and diligence were conducted.

Kingsbridge was in full-on acquisition mode with their

interest intensifying daily. Late-night calls from the CEO and Chairman Charles Green were common. (In 2012, Green's consortium was identified as the preferred bidder for Glasgow Rangers FC, who were in administration at the time).

As the interest intensified, an offer was not far away. I knew little of what to expect having only been in operation for a year. Despite my rapid rise to stardom, this was new ground for me. Mark kept me informed on progress until the offer arrived. We now discovered what was on the table.

£2,500,000.

* * *

The offer filled me with pride. With only 12 months of trade behind us, the notion that an outfit of the stature of Kingsbridge was prepared to commit two and a half million pounds to buy my company was incredible. Even back then, around the turn of the new millennium, the sum represented a staggering amount of money. My mind once again drifted back over my past, as I reflected on the rejections and putdowns I had encountered earlier in my career. I would never make a success of myself, I was assured.

£2,500,000 didn't seem like a bad response to my earlier critics.

As the talks continued, I agreed to sign the deal. Mark did a great job in checking over the intricate details of the contract for me. The package would result in my relinquishing ownership rights of the company and working for Kingsbridge PLC for an initial minimum term of three years (the "earn-out period.") I would receive an annual salary of £85,000 (which is equivalent to a six-figure sum these days), company car and bonuses, etc.

Plus, the small matter of £2.5million of course.

A date was set for me to attend the company's stockbroker office in the city of London. Attendees would include the board of directors, Kingsbridge's stockbroking team, myself, and Mark.

Mark and I arrived at the offices of Teather & Greenwood

stockbrokers, for the meeting. The scene resembled one from a big, Hollywood blockbuster movie.

A table surrounded by sharp-suited businessmen with champagne on ice, in anticipation of celebrating the multi million pound deal.

We learned how Kingsbridge's expansion plans were well underway, with share values steadily climbing. The press announcement which would follow my signing of the deal would see share prices rise further, to the benefit of us all. This was the stuff of dreams, as my acceptance of the deal would bring millionaire status. The offer would include a mixture of shares and cash.

As the moment of signing drew near though, I sensed some reticence coming across from Mark. He asked Kingsbridge for a moment's respite. A "time out" as our American cousins might describe it.

The mood around the table shifted tangibly as Mark sought a brief, private moment with me.

To my astonishment, Mark advised me that he felt I should not sign. I was selling myself short, he argued. My earning potential and business acumen far exceeded what was on offer, he felt.

Blinking in disbelief, I treated Mark to a five-minute synopsis of my life. The humble origins in deepest Pembrokeshire, scuttling around on a bike delivering telegrams, rejection, dismay from teachers, and managers, etc. I was the original country cousin, with money now on the table from Kingsbridge to turn me into a real city gent for life. I was not in the habit of rejecting multi-million-pound deals, I advised my trusted counsellor.

The atmosphere back in the meeting room was now one of tension and silence. The life-changing paperwork sat staring up at me. Untold riches lay just a signature away.

My heart began to race as the voices inside my head went into overdrive. The voices echoed Mark's reticence.

"They fear you, Jon. You are their competition."

"Don't sign. Don't sign!"

Mark was right, I concluded. This had all come about too quickly. My future was mine to make, not Kingsbridge's. These were my dreams, not yours, I told myself. I had more left in me. More to invest in me, not a future waiting to be signed away to a room full of men in grey suits one Friday evening.

The consequences of my deliberations would go on to occupy my mind that whole weekend as I contemplated what I did. My head would be in a spin, but a new determination would see me focused on making my own life successful. On making my own dreams come true.

A stony silence anticipated my inevitable decision.

"No deal."

Going the Extra Mile

I knew that it was time to move on from Kingsbridge.

I confess that the offer turned my head, but I remained fully focused on building, developing, and maintaining my business, as did my staff. My hobby was my business, and my business was my hobby. I had sacrificed so much to establish my enterprise as one of the best in its field.

Life found me in a different city each day. London, Birmingham, Manchester, Portsmouth. At times it resembled a top football club fulfilling its gruelling fixture list!

Travelling around the country for client meetings meant that it was far from an office-based existence. Chantell ran things back at base. She was also a qualified Independent Financial Adviser in her own right. She supported my clients along with the other advisers who we always had on board, the best of them being Jonathan Richards, Robbie Weston, and Gary McMorran.

Charlotte, Kim and Kelly were also vital cogs in the machinery through the provision of administrative backup and support to a growing client base. The staff were well rewarded and enjoyed a fulfilling role, rubbing shoulders with our high-profile clients.

Motivating, encouraging, and developing the staff were key drivers for me back then. I can't over-emphasise the importance of a strong team behind the scenes at all levels. People are the most important asset any organisation has, and it was critical that the staff shared my vision. The whole team performed with me at a hectic pace to deliver a joined-up, quality service for our clients.

At this point, it might prove helpful to explain the nature of the contractual relationship between Jonathan Power Associates and our clients.

Clients were not 'contracted' exclusively to us. They would all be free to use any other company at any time.

It was crucial that we were "on the ball" so to speak and

providing a top-of-the-table service to clients. All being well, our clients would be pleased to stay on our books and even refer us to potential new contacts. Word-of-mouth recommendations played a big part in the expansion of our business. It sounds simple but the important contribution that played in our success is hard to overstate.

As our reputation spread, a domino effect kicked in as the relationships we established paved the way for more business. We put ourselves firmly within the 'inner circle' of financial services and A-List clients.

To explain how the service operated, let's imagine that a client wanted a particular type of investment opportunity. I sat down with them to establish their goals. Pension advice? ISA? Investment opportunities? We covered the full gambit of financial opportunities. Were they looking for high returns, easy access, or both? For how long were they looking to invest? Would the policy mature when their playing days ended; what about injuries?

I would take all this information away and provide a detailed report on the best available products to meet their needs. Our income would come in the form of commissions from the various financial institutions with whom our clients invested. The clients didn't pay any money for our advice, which made us extremely popular! Rigid "compliance checks" ensured that the solutions we produced were 100% credible and suited to the needs of the clients.

With the sort of sums these guys were willing to invest, it was crucial that we signposted them to the best opportunities. Establishing, maintaining, and developing our reputation within the market was a 24/7 commitment. The importance of relationships we built with the financial sector was easily the single factor in our success, as we brokered a wide range of financial opportunities. That reputation fed back to the service we could offer our clients. The domino effect, as I say.

The arrangements which governed our relationships with clients did not commit them to sign up for any specific term or timescale. This flexibility appealed significantly to the nature of our client base. Steve Staunton, the former Liverpool, Aston Villa, and Republic of Ireland defender, told the 2003/04 PFA Footballers' 'who's who' that Jonathan Power Associates Limited were "experts in their field."

Though I say so myself, Steve was right. Our expertise was underpinned by access to every bank, building society, insurance company, investment company and mortgage lender. Mortgage advice, re-mortgage advice, pension planning, tax planning, car finance, life assurance and even will writing. It really was the most comprehensive of services.

Some of the clients were just starting out on their career path and some were at the pinnacle of their careers. However, they all appreciated the secure, professional, and friendly service we offered as we gained their trust and respect. Our clients had been accustomed to the world of football agents etc. Men of money with poker faces. They would commit clients to fixed-term undertakings. Any breakdown in the relationship between player and agent would simply see the agent point to "para 12(b)(iii) (as amended)" of their agreement and ensure that the player stayed put, as per contract.

Your average sports star is not normally renowned for their hard-nosed business acumen or expertise in navigating complex contractual terms. Our simple 'take it or leave it' offer struck a chord with them. Clients were free to simply stay or go. Most stayed.

I collaborated with many top agents in those days and yes, there were many opportunities to become an agent myself. This would have led to significant conflicts of interest with my financial services provider of course. I'd have been riding two horses in the same race. The impact on my ability to offer that 'independence' that I valued so deeply would have been significantly compromised. Agents would never have recommended me to their own clients for independent advice if they thought that I had an 'inner circle' of clients who I represented myself and whose interests I sought to advance.

Integrity, like justice, must not only be done but it must also be seen to be done.

In later years though, I did represent certain clients as their agent. I enjoyed my time in that dog-eat-dog world and became a real-life Jerry McGuire. "Show me the money!"

Many of my clients were top-drawer names from the world of professional football. We supported the absolute best.

I worked with all manner of agents for my clients. Former footballers such as ex-Chelsea and Scotland striker David Speedie, the former Millwall, Newport, and Watford favourite Jamie Moralee and the one-time Wolves striker, Mel Eves. Israeli agent David Abou and football scout Peter Miles were also great supporters of my organisation.

Eves is an interesting example, as, upon leaving the game, he also became an independent financial advisor (IFA) often advising young footballers. The mid-90s saw him become a licensed FA agent, although also running an IFA business.

In later years he represented high-profile players such as Enzo Maresca, Benito Carbone, the silver-haired Fabrizio Ravanelli, Wales star Robert Earnshaw and Northern Ireland international Gareth McAuley. That's quite a line-up. Former England boss Roy Hodgson has been fulsome of his praise for McAuley as one of his best-ever signings by the way. Gareth later became a client on the recommendation of Mel Eves.

Others came from a business background, accountants and such. Men like Jon Smith, who headed up First Artist, a company floated on the stock market. Jon was one of the best in the business whose clients had included top pop stars. I dealt with his staff in the main, who included the towering Steve Wicks (former Chelsea captain who also turned out for Derby, QPR, and Crystal Palace) and Matthew Francis, son of Trevor, Britain's first million-pound footballer you may recall.

We took great pride in going that extra mile for these guys. They certainly appreciated the level of service we delivered. Often, on hearing that I would not represent them myself, players would ask me to recommend an agent. This resulted in many referrals to agents, all of which went down well. Some long-standing relationships grew from this between players and agents. This 'relationship building' role is hard to measure or quantify but, again, proved critical to my success. That 'word of mouth' thing.

I never asked for commission in linking players with agents but the impact on my reputation added to my worth as a trusted confidant. It added value to the relationship between our clients and the organisation. Business is business, yes, but you can't just chase the Yankee dollar. Sometimes you must build trust, confidence, and integrity. Then maybe the benefits will come. In my case, in time, they certainly came.

It's hard work that doesn't show up in the end-of-year accounting statements. It manifested itself though in the establishment and expansion of the company.

I recall many occasions when an individual or agent would refer their own clients to my company. Inevitably this sometimes resulted in the odd spot of humour and even confusion.

Picture the scene. London. A London taxi. One of the iconic, big black numbers. The London traffic careering all around us, carving us up as the steely-eyed taxi driver held his nerve. He did this every day after all. White knuckles in the passenger seat.

As best as I can recall, my appointment was with Andy Frampton, a player from Crystal Palace. South of the river. I enjoyed some good business relationships with many of the guys down at Selhurst Park in those days. This engagement was set for the Croydon Park Hotel CR9 5AA, an impressive venue boasting all the attractions you might expect of such an establishment.

Along the journey through the hectic London streets, my phone, as ever, rang constantly. It was difficult when there were third parties around (aka the taxi driver) and inevitably, he picked up the odd snatch of conversation with my clients. It aroused his curiosity.

"So, what do you do for a living then boss?" he inquired. I muttered something about giving advice to footballers, more focussed on the clock than the chat.

During the ensuing conversation, it emerged that he had a mate who he considered to be a half-decent footballer. "Oh aye," I half interestingly responded, anticipating a story about some lump of a striker who plied their trade on Hackney Marshes. My chauffeur explained that the guy was a fellow African, but I remained unimpressed really. I needed to be at Croydon Park. I had heard a million tales of "talented" youngsters and their goal-scoring feats in junior football. Their proud parents were all convinced that I should sign them up with Chelsea, Man United, or Liverpool. Some parents can be like that.

To 'close the deal' (in other words, to get into the hotel to meet my client), I scribbled down the taxi driver's number. I stuffed it into my pocket like you would with some girl you just met in a club, and dashed into Croydon Park.

The meeting with Andy went well. He appreciated the advice I offered and remained with the company. Smiles and handshakes all around. The eagle had landed.

In the ensuing days though, somehow, curiosity got the better of me. For a reason I remain unable to articulate, I found myself fumbling about in my pockets for the receipt for the journey on which I had written the name of the taxi driver. In a speculative mood, I took a punt on ringing a dependable contact of mine, Andy Evans, CEO of World in Motion sporting agency. Andy laughed with me at the story but, hey, he would ring the driver when time permitted. Andy would keep me in the loop but really, I thought little more of the whole episode.

A short time elapsed. I heard from Andy. Not only had he spoken to the driver of my taxi but, it seems, had arranged a trial for the mystery footballer. The trial would be with Bristol Rovers, managed back then by the colourful Ian Holloway. The player would need to cover his own expenses and travel costs. The Pirates weren't pushing the boat out by any means. The player duly showed up at the trial. No one really knew what to expect, or even expected much.

Holloway was from Kingswood, a suburban town in South Gloucestershire, England, bordering the eastern edge of

Bristol. He called the agent.

"What the hell have you sent me?" he rasped, in those instantly recognisable, almost exaggerated West Country tones.

Expecting the worst, Andy commenced his mitigation.

"Some you win. Some you lose boss."

"It was just a shot in the dark Ian."

The Bristolian gaffer explained how the entire experience had been one of embarrassment for his players. I could feel Andy cursing me from down the M4.

The African had (and I quote) "taken the piss" out of his boys in their own backyard.

For yes, it turns out that the mate of my taxi driver was simply a talent on another level from – with all due respect – the mighty Bristol Rovers. Holloway would love to have signed him up for The Gas but knew that the player was simply in another class.

Holloway, therefore, contacted Watford Boss Graham Taylor. A respected figure in the game. He was keen to let Taylor know all about the African jewel which had dropped into his lap.

It turned out, inevitably, that our find was no chancer from the Sunday Morning leagues of South London. It was Ben Iroha, who featured in two World Cups, won the Africa Cup of Nations, and went on to earn 50 caps for Nigeria before embarking on a coaching career.

Note to self: Always listen to your taxi driver.

I was pleased to have played a small part in Ben's story. All I did really was simply move the story along though. Wheels within wheels.

Graham Taylor signed Iroha in a heartbeat having seen him play. From taxicab to Premier League. A remarkable story.

Ben and I remain good friends to this day. As I say, the odd phone call here, a quiet word there. Sometimes, just being a voice on the end of the phone. You won't find these items showing up on any balance sheet but, trust me, they have their worth.

Just ask Ben Iroha.

I worked on the basis of referral and recommendation, as I

have said. Regular, positive media coverage ensured that my company remained in the public eye. We had little need to advertise. The local hacks liked us but we also saw our fair share of coverage in the nationals – the *News of the World* and *Sunday Times* for example.

Ben also became one of our clients, thanks perhaps to the small part I had played in his 'discovery.' At one of our early encounters, Ben let it be known that the Ambassador of Sport in Nigeria wanted to meet me. Super Ben set up the rendezvous for the 4-star Selfridge Hotel – a venue in the heart of London.

Imagine my surprise when the Ambassador turned out to be none other than John Fashanu, the former Wimbledon star. He of Crazy Gang fame!

I must confess I had never really pictured Fash as your typical diplomat, but Ambassador Fashanu was immensely proud of his role.

Strange to think that that random conversation in a taxicab should unravel such a story for us all. So many business connections sprang from what was just a passing word." The thought you had in a taxicab" as Odyssey once sang. A simple act of thoughtfulness that could have got left on the curb. They say that God moves in mysterious ways, don't they?

Fash became a great champion of my company. An ambassador, even. Many of his associates became clients.

The former striker also helped me find a property in London when I was looking to buy. This support featured the best financial advice I would ever receive, and helped set me on the road to establishing my way in the field of property investment.

I stayed in London quite regularly in those days you see, always at the Selfridge Hotel, where I would be looked after well. Concierge car-parking, all the trappings of success I suppose. It became both a second home and a business base, as many of my client meetings took place there.

It was all part of the package. I had to show my credibility to my clients. The suit I wore, the car I drove, the watch on my wrist. It was all part of my toolkit which showed my clients that I was at home in their world.

Anyway, being unfamiliar with the geography of the capital, I stuck to what I knew, despite the hefty accommodation bills that were being run up.

Around this time, Ambassador Fashanu put me in touch with his own property adviser, who represented several high-profile clients and enjoyed connections with leading City estate agents. Before long, a suitable property was located, a one-bedroomed apartment in a gated private development in Brook Green, an affluent neighbourhood that stands at the end of Kensington High Street in the London Borough of Hammersmith and Fulham.

As far as I understood at the time, the property was the subject of a 'forced sale,' possibly arising from a divorce settlement or repossession proceedings. The property adviser put forward by John Fashanu had developed an eye for seeking out such opportunities it seemed. His fees were added to the asking price, which was then ultimately, passed to the buyer. In this case, me of course. This was known as "flipping" the property apparently. It is also known as "wholesale real estate investing," a real estate investment strategy whereby an investor acquires a property not to use, but with the intention of selling it for profit. The focus is generally on speed as opposed to maximum profit.

Even allowing for the add-on fees though, there remained plenty of value in this desirable property in an attractive part of London. At £185,000 the price was certainly beneath market value. I stumped up the cash.

The apartment proved to be my home in London. My base. A place I could call my own. Mortgage charges were a fraction of the outlay I had been used to in hotel fees etc. Ok, I now had to park my own car, but you can't have everything!

I was in good company it seems, as former England football manager Terry Venables had also once occupied the development. I was happy to take that as an endorsement of the address!

Within a year, the property doubled in value. It turned out to be a fabulous investment. I even recommended that adviser to clients of mine who completed several similar transactions. I couldn't help thinking back to that taxi ride. Talk about seizing the moment. Backing your instincts. Sometimes "the race is not to the swift or the battle to the strong, for time and chance happen to them all." (Ecclesiastes 9:11.) I made the chance. It may have been a lucky punt but sometimes you must make your own luck. My dad taught me that.

Throughout my time as an Independent Financial Adviser, I always operated based on referrals and recommendations. Teammates would refer me to teammates, agents would pass on my details to their clients, and scouting networks would pick up on the scent. Word soon spread around the Premier League dressing rooms. The world of football can be a small one at times, and it was common for me to represent several members of the same team.

This began back in the early days and through my association with my hometown club, Cardiff City, then managed by Eddie May.

Eddie was a great bloke bless him and a valued client. He referred several of the Cardiff lads to me for advice. Lads like experienced full-back Damon Searle (shame Damon never earned a cap for Wales), towering young centre-back Lee Baddley, the highly engaging former Manchester United player Derek Brazil and fellow defender Scott Young. The Flying Postman John Williams was also a client. He earned the nickname due to his pace and career before football. Also on my books were Welsh Internationals Daniel Gabbidon, Rob Earnshaw, Jason Perry, and the exceptionally talented Mark Delaney – who moved from the humble environment of Carmarthen Town to Aston Villa via Ninian Park for the fee of £500,000. That was a hefty sum for a club like Cardiff City then.

Some of these 'local hero' players went on to become household names in the higher echelons of the game and enjoyed good careers. The same principles which I learned and applied back then continued to serve me well throughout my career. It didn't matter whether I was advising journeymen stalwarts from the lower divisions or Premier League legends who would lift the top trophies in the game.

I often referred players to other agents who I thought would be suitable. An example of this was when Ben Iroha once asked me to represent Jay-Jay Okocha, the talented Nigerian former professional footballer who eventually turned out 73 times for the Nigeria national team.

Jay-Jay was arguably one of the most talented players at the time. He was on the books at Paris St. Germain and I had two meetings with him in Paris. For one meeting I brought in two representatives of First Artist – Steve Wicks and Matthew Francis. Okocha didn't sign with First Artist in the end and chose to stick with his own advisers. This led to a move to the unlikely outpost of Bolton Wanderers.

With all due respect to The Trotters, there is no doubt in my mind that First Artist would have secured a move to send the Nigerian start to a top Premier League team. One capable of providing the showcase that his talents deserved.

Top agents do the big deals, and this is just as relevant today as it was then. Connecting people to people in this way was a major part of my business strategy.

He continues to enjoy global fame and was appointed to join other football legends in April 2022 as draw assistants for the FIFA 2022 World Cup in Qatar. Okocha joined Germany's Lothar Matthaüs, Brazil's Cafu, Algeria's Rabah Madjer, Australia's Tim Cahill, Qatari's Adel Ahmed MalAllah, and Iran's Ali Daei. They were all joined by the coach of the Super Eagles at the 1998 World Cup, Bora Milutinovic.

I can't help thinking of the positive impact I could have had on his club career though, had he taken maximum advantage of the connections I was able to offer.

Here are just some of the other star football names we worked with:

Manchester United: Andrew Cole, Rio Ferdinand, Michael Carrick.

Chelsea: John Terry, Joe Cole, Jody Morris, Michael

Duberry.

Leicester City: Muzzy Izzet, Matthew Jones, Robbie Savage.

Liverpool: David James, Craig Bellamy, Salif Diao.

There are a few medals and international caps in that lot aren't there – and that's just a selection of the names we worked with. We reached for the stars – and the stars teamed up with us.

We represented all types of players at all types of clubs. We had a good record of creating relationships with stars who would go on to reach considerable heights in the game. Mostly. Down on the South Coast at Portsmouth FC, we advised stars such as Scottish international Nigel Quashie – one of a handful of players who turned out for both Pompey and Southampton, Shaun Derry – a tough-tackling midfielder who played over 500 games in his career – and the former Arsenal junior Jason Crowe. Decent players with creditable CVs. Darren Moore was also a client of mine.

I was proud to work with Darren – a man of strong faith who is active in the Christian charity Faith and Football – and I am so pleased that he enjoys the reputation that he does in the modern game. It is richly deserved for the man whose career saw him chalk up over 600 games, including 60+ for Pompey.

A referral came through for me to pop along for a chat with another player who had recently signed for Pompey. At the player's request, I made contact and set up a rendezvous. I thought little of it. These were busy times for our organisation, with a growing client list to support as well as our existing players of course.

To my slight surprise, at the conclusion of our first meeting, the player indicated that he would like to speak to his mother before engaging the services of a financial adviser. I respected this from a young man – Mum knows best after all – though I must admit that it wasn't quite the response I was used to from the calibre of clients that we normally encountered. I didn't lose much sleep over any delay it might cause though, given the already extensive demands on our time from our expanding list of clients. I wasn't going to force the pace with any hard sell either. That was never my style.

I had to decide on this one though. Should I push for another meeting or just write it off as the deal-that-never-was with a player-that-never-would-be? I thought of asking an intermediary such as Sir Geoff Hurst to intercede on my behalf, to assure the player (and his mum) that we are a genuine outfit that could be relied upon to provide the sort of independent financial advice that could be of benefit. I don't recall John Terry or Rio Ferdinand being as cautious as this guy but I guess it takes all sorts.

I also wasn't wholly convinced that this unlikely-looking guy could expect much of a future in the game, to be honest. I decided to write it off and concentrate my efforts elsewhere. We had other elite clients who surely would offer more to the game. I decided not to pursue it.

Oh… and the identity of this striker for whom I saw no future? Peter Crouch.

***

Notwithstanding the occasional lack of judgement such as this though, overall, these were extremely rewarding and fulfilling times for me.

John Fashanu had now also become a client and a real champion of my company. He put a considerable amount of his own free time into the company. He always believed that we exceeded clients' expectations and went above and beyond what would normally be expected. For example, I recall his astonishment that we did not charge mortgage arrangement fees, unlike other firms. We also provided a complimentary accounting service for our clients, at considerable personal cost to myself I might add.

John tells a story of how we once advised the big man to insure his legs for £500,000. After one season at Aston Villa, Fash went into a tackle with Ryan Giggs and the Welshman's boot caught his right knee, snapping the medial ligaments. John describes how a few months later he was forced to retire but cites how "Jonathan's wisdom was invaluable. The insurance company paid out the £500,000."

I must admit I don't quite recognise or recall my involvement in these events, but thanks for the endorsement Fash! It got my name in the *Sunday Times* anyway.

Fashanu had tried to invest in Northampton Town with the help of a Nigerian benefactor who he said was like a father to him, Chief Sonny Odogwu, who was also chairman of Winners Worldwide, a football agency that Fashanu fronted. When the £3 million deal failed to materialise, he turned his attention to Barry Town.

To the uninitiated out there, Barry Town FC might take a little explaining. Barry Town – Barry as in Gavin & Stacey yes – was a semi-professional association football team who competed at the League of Wales level. In their heyday they enjoyed considerable success, beating Cardiff City in the Welsh Cup Final at the old Cardiff Arms Park in 1994 and achieving a hat trick of cup wins at the start of the new millennium. Between 1996 and 2003 they won the league 7 times.

This brought considerable exposure and European nights against Aberdeen and Porto. Barry, therefore, represented Wales in Europe during the 90s and early 2000s. They were the Manchester United or even Real Madrid of the league for some time. Despite playing at what some consider to be a 'non-league' level, Fashanu clearly saw the potential for this type of venture and became Chairman of the club.

The former Crazy Gang star even asked if I would be interested in joining the Barry board, drawing on my earlier experience perhaps as a director at Newport AFC, a club that eventually morphed into a 'new' Newport County. It was an interesting offer but, ultimately, one which I declined. Whilst there was undoubted potential at Jenner Park (the home of Barry Town) I couldn't help thinking that it wasn't quite the role for me. Attendances at the time were poor and whilst football at that level has made considerable strides, with media exposure to match, I still felt that it wasn't an opportunity that really called out to me. I had to think about the impartiality of my business too of course.

John vacated the role in 2003. It's a shame that the deal never quite took off in the way that he might have hoped, as Barry have a loyal, enthusiastic fan base and play at a decent stadium that has the physical potential for development. More and more former Welsh internationals have moved to League of Wales clubs in recent years as players and managers (the Cymru Premier as it later became known – Cymru being Welsh for Wales of course.) Who knows, perhaps one day Barry Town really will cross swords with Manchester United or Real Madrid in European action?

Occasionally, of course, the seeds we planted fell on stony ground. You can lead a horse to water but...

For example, I recall how, at the insistence of my company patron Sir Bobby Robson, I met Paul Gascoigne along with his agent Wes Saunders at the 5-star Ritz Hotel in Mayfair, London.

As my organisation grew and we expanded our services, we began promoting a remarkable, fashionable development at Chelsea Bridge Wharf in London SW8, in association with Berkeley Homes and New Era Wealth Management. Sir Bobby himself had endorsed the development of luxury properties. "Their quality and investment appeal, especially to my colleagues in the sports industry, is exceptional," he said. The site was close to top London retail environments and cosmopolitan attractions.

Sir Bobby wanted Paul to invest and buy an apartment that he could call his own in this prestigious development. The complex offered security measures, CCTV, a concierge service, and a host of other design features. It would have suited Gazza down to the ground, giving him a secure city centre environment and the privacy which he had earned.

Also in attendance during the discussion was Paul's wife, Cheryl, though they were no longer living together then. The fatherly Sir Bobby felt that Gazza should have a place of his own that he could call home.

I was shocked at Gazza's appearance. Smoking nervously

and constantly throughout our meeting, he resembled a shadow of his former self. He had aged since I first met him and his demeanour now was sad to see. The whole of the football world loves Gazza. In his day, it had not been hard to see why.

Sir Bobby, Wes Saunders, and Gazza himself were very keen to go ahead with the investment. It was clear though that Cheryl had her doubts, for reasons only she would know. The last thing I wanted was to become embroiled in any Gascoigne v Gascoigne drama, so I stepped away and just waited for a callback. I left it to Gazza to call me if the deal was to be resurrected. It was a great opportunity for the jovial Geordie.

The call never came.

I always tried to support my clients whenever I had a chance to see them in action. "Going the extra mile" as I say.

On one occasion, I took a flight to Spain, where Liverpool was taking on Barcelona in Champions League action. All the pre-match talk before the first leg of their last-16 tie had centred around a bust-up between Craig Bellamy and John Arne Riise.

Come the game itself, both Bellars and the Norwegian got on the scoresheet to secure a famous win for the Reds. The Anfield men had fallen behind but Bellamy grabbed the equaliser just before half time then the fiery Welshman set up Riise for the 74th-minute winner. Bellamy celebrated by swinging an imaginary golf club. You can look up the significance of that gesture yourself!

The story was a memorable one for me though as, prior to the game, international household name Craig Bellamy had asked me to pop out and buy him a new pair of boots. Honest! Size 6 as I recall. I am sure they were Nike. I duly obliged. Anything for a client.

To then watch my compatriot turn it on in front of 88,000 at the Nou Camp against the Catalan Giants was a great thrill. Lionel Messi, Iniesta, and Ronaldinho all turned out for Barca that night, but Cardiff-born Bellamy and his new boots were just too good for 'em. Bellissimo.

Maybe I should have claimed an assist?

To continue the golfing reference, this kind of escapade just seemed par for the course. My relationships with my clients are often way beyond the traditional role, though I must admit, a shopping trip to buy Bellars' boots probably takes some beating.

On another occasion, I attended a match at Stamford Bridge, the London home of Chelsea FC. Everton were the opponents. Tickets for the best seats in the house at this lunchtime kick-off were provided to me by a player. Nothing unusual there. I took along a friend as a guest, Jon Dando, a big Toffees fan. We drove up on the day of the game, due to meet the wives at Soho House later for dinner.

As we drove to the game, contemplating the usual London traffic and its potential to make me late for the kick-off, my phone rang. The caller enquired whether I was still ok to attend the fixture as time was pressing. I hadn't yet picked up my tickets, he reminded me.

To the astonishment of Dando, the caller was Blues skipper John Terry. For it was he who had secured the precious tickets,

I advised the Chelsea captain of my predicament amidst the Saturday morning London traffic but assured him that I would make the fixture and meet up with him afterwards in the players' bar. A man who won almost every major honour in the game and captained club and country could relax ahead of the game now, safe in the knowledge that J Power from Pembrokeshire would be ok to make it to the game. He probably only had about 45 minutes left before kick-off, yet here he was ringing me up over match tickets.

The result of that Everton clash has faded from memory now. Many football fans will tell you that the actual 90 minutes is often the least significant part of any football trip. I would even struggle to recall the date. My overriding memory of the day is not any spectacular winner from Frank Lampard or a piledriver free kick from Leighton Baines, it is the memory of one of the most respected footballers of his day showing consideration that I would be able to collect his tickets in time and take an old friend to the match.

JT. Top man.

It's just the kind of anecdote that made the whole show worthwhile.

Two Sirs

My career brought me into close contact with a host of celebrities.

In my early days, I advised lower league footballers and sporting personalities whose fame may not have extended far beyond the city walls of Cardiff or the shores of my native Wales.

In later years though, I encountered a wider clientele and impressive business associates. International figures, household names, stars of stage and screen. Names known on Broadway and in Hollywood. Even royalty.

I hope that I came to represent them all with grace, dignity, and integrity. It was important not to be overawed when sitting at the negotiating table with figures who were heroes to many.

The biggest names from the association football and rugby union. Top pop acts. World champions in boxing and snooker. Big names, with a record of achievement to match. Their very name was their calling card. The last thing they needed was an overawed youngster overseeing their weighty financial affairs. Earning and maintaining the respect of my clients was a major driver for me. I had to show these guys that I knew my stuff. Demonstrating that I led a team with the experience and credibility to match their aspirations was always critical to our success.

Yes, of course though, it was a thrill sometimes to rub shoulders with Premier League stars and other famous faces. Some inevitably left a lasting impression on this bright-eyed Pembrokeshire lad.

Perhaps it was because of their success or their standing in the sports or entertainment community. I may have been moved by their achievements, and the respect they commanded beyond their immediate world. Sometimes even, all of the above. Figures whose reputation, personality, and standing, set them apart from others.

Stars of their firmament.
Like these two.
Starry, starry Knights.

Sir Geoff.

Sir Geoffrey Charles Hurst MBE is a name known across the globe. He remains, of course, the only man to score a hat trick in a World Cup Final. Pele, Maradona, Cruyff. Messi and Ronaldo even. None of these ever managed it. Geoff Hurst's fame for those three strikes puts him alongside the biggest names in world football. The biggest names in history, some would say, given the impact of the achievements of the boys of 66 on the growth of the beautiful game in England and probably even the world.

1966 and all that.

Hurst scored around 250 goals throughout his entire career, appearing for West Ham United, Stoke City, West Bromwich Albion, and of course England. Those three famous Wembley strikes though, have cemented his fame in schoolboy scrapbooks, pub quizzes and football almanacs for almost 60 years.

And they always will.

Kenneth Wolstenholme's famous "they think it's all over commentary" line, cemented that hat-trick into broadcasting history, immortalising Sir Geoff within popular culture. Even the linesman who considered that second goal to be over the line has a stadium named after him in Baku, Azerbaijan.

In the 60s, Sir Geoff Hurst of West Ham United was also named "Hammer of the Year" three times – another hat trick.

My first contact with the Wembley hero arose through a mutual female associate in Selfridges Hotel. Andrea was well known to the Boys of 66 and often assisted them with event management affairs etc. At times, Selfridges virtually served as additional office accommodation for me back then. Selfridges were more than pleased to let me set up regular camp in one of their rooms, in exchange for the kudos arising from the celebrity footfall I delivered. After all, it's not exactly negative publicity to have Sir Geoff Hurst spotted in your lobby, is it?

I saw Sir Geoff as the ideal figurehead for my company, Jonathan Power Associates Limited. We already advised a host of top football figures as well as rugby stars, boxers, and pop idols. He could be the ambassador whose name, reputation, and fame would send out a positive public image of JPA.

Sir Geoff had been knighted in 1998 in the Queen's Birthday Honours List for services to sport. He would give real credibility to our company, which already enjoyed a strong reputation. The part-time role would see him feature in marketing and publicity information. He would take part in presentations to groups of prospective clients and act as an 'introducer.' PR work and public appearances would help promote the business; the odd speaking engagement perhaps and lots of handshakes. Who wouldn't want their photo taken with Sir Geoff Hurst?

The tormentor of West Germany seemed very taken with me. In an intense two hour meeting, he wanted to find out all about me. What was my business acumen like? What was my philosophy? What did my parents even do? What made me "tick?"

There was little room for small talk in that initial encounter, which was a full-on business discussion as I sold myself and my company to one of the most famous names in sporting history. At no time did the subject of 1966 even remotely arise. No opportunity for me to ask about his famous football feats.

The meeting was intense, but Sir Geoff was approachable and dignified throughout. He knew his worth and was fully aware of the strength of his name. There was no sense of aloofness though about this dedicated family man, who treated me with the utmost respect throughout.

We discussed remuneration of course, though I recall that my offer did not feel to me like a significant sum to a man of his standing. When you are a national hero, it seems, commercial offers are never far away. He was clearly a man in constant demand. Many of the approaches he received were declined. I was sceptical as to whether he would accept my modest, non-executive offer, for his financial status now greatly exceeded the reported weekly wage of £45 he had collected back in 1966!

Sir Geoff was a sought-after dinner guest who held a significant ambassadorial role with the Football Association, acting as one of England's ambassadors in the bid to host the World Cup in 2006. For many years, he also held the post of Director of Football with McDonald's. His other associates included Chase de Vere Mortgage Management. Huge business partners. To have a name like his on board could mean so much. His name and reputation would give us the competitive edge and 'star quality' to set us apart from our competitors, of whom there were many. His name would turn heads for sure.

We discussed terms, including a percentage of the value of the company if we ever sold up. His secretary would call me with his decision, he announced, ending our intense discussions. I feared a "no" but at least I had given it my best shot. I had sought to create the opportunity. My parents would be satisfied with that.

The following day, my mobile phone rang. It was Sir Geoff himself. The England hero had been extremely impressed with my performance, enthusiasm, and ability. He had enjoyed our exchange. He wished to accept my offer with immediate effect. Sir Geoff Hurst MBE would join the board of Jonathan Power Associates Ltd as a non-executive director.

I was ecstatic.

Sir Geoff later explained just why he had accepted a role with our company.

He had recognised how JPA could help well-paid players maintain and develop their worth when the time came to hang up their boots. He knew the value of good, impartial advice from people who understood the needs of modern, highly paid, international household names. He recognised that our clients could trust our advice, for impartiality would also be key. Players should avoid advice sources tied to one company. Our ability to offer independent financial advice across the whole marketplace was an important ace in our pack.

This was news worth sharing. The Sports Café in Haymarket was selected as the venue for a press launch, deep in the heart of the English capital. Recognising the high-end image which our company now carried, the venue offered its facilities free of charge. Drinks and nibbles would be complementary, in exchange for sharing the gloss emanating from names like Sir Geoff Hurst. What was that about my business acumen, Geoff?

Our business was still in its infancy mind, and my small team running the outfit really were jacks of all trades. Without the resources of a PR department yet, I took to contacting various press agencies and media outlets. It was all hands to the pump in those days. I probably even made the odd cup of tea for everyone!

We took over the entire downstairs of the Sports Café one afternoon with an enormous contingent of press representatives in attendance. Many of those present weren't invited by me. Sir Geoff was on board. Word of mouth had done the rest. JPA had pluckily tossed our pebble into the pond and now the ripples were spreading, gathering pace as the press and others caught up with the waves we were creating. The event was a 'closed door' function though so many representatives found their way in. Journalists and representatives from the heart of the London scene. The event was a great success.

We were then subsequently invited to attend a drinks reception, organised by a third party, as news of the venture spread quickly. The festivities moved to Soho House. If I ever needed a demonstration of the power and respect which accompanied the name of Sir Geoff Hurst, this was a strong example.

Sir Geoff was unable to attend this second function, but I was happy enough to show up. Boy was that a good call. The media and glitterati once again filed the prestigious venue, a Grade II listed townhouse in Greek Street. These days Soho House has venues across the globe. This exclusive establishment, founded in 1995, has a long waiting list for potential new members, though, amazingly, I was offered immediate membership. Madonna once threw a party at the venue. Prince Harry and Meghan Markle enjoyed their first date at this Soho establishment.

Strict restrictions were in place to preserve the privacy and dignity of such exalted names. No photographs, video footage or autographs here.

I quickly became further embroiled in the London scene and Sir Geoff and I kept in regular touch, even exchanging Christmas cards.

He quickly became a key part of our business life, meeting my staff. Signed biographies were made available to the team. He met my own family as this Wembley legend became a huge factor in our image and success, proving a tremendous link to the press. These were immensely proud times for me as I saw our potential growth.

Sir Geoff was impressed with our set-up. I am sure he also cast an admiring glance or two around the sports memorabilia adorning my office walls when he visited on one occasion in March 2004. That collection of signed shirts came from some of the many international football stars that I had represented.

As we sat chatting over business affairs, I heard a knock at the door. It was my father. I introduced one to another, though I suspect that Dad probably already recognised Geoff Hurst, the 1966 hero.

Dad jumped straight in. No hesitation. "Tell me, Geoff, did the ball really cross the line?" I wilted with embarrassment. Oh Dad, you just don't do that!

Sir Geoff must have been asked this countless times before. It felt like the equivalent of "can we have a selfie, Geoff." Would he take offence?

To his eternal credit though, Sir Geoff Hurst, 49 England caps and a Knight of the Realm, acted with customary dignity and grace. "Mr Power" he responded, "I will tell you what happened."

Sir Geoff Hurst then spent the next half an hour taking my father – and myself – through every step of that goal, describing how he had hit Alan Ball's cross in movement, tumbling backwards in the process. His shot had hit the bar and rebounded to the floor.

The West German defence headed the ball clear. The English side claimed a goal, believing that the shot had landed over the line. Liverpool's Roger Hunt had been in close attendance. He would have followed up the shot if he had thought it hadn't crossed the whitewash, wouldn't he? The linesman from Azerbaijan concurred with the men in red. Three Lions on their chest. The Swiss referee awarded a goal. 3-2 England. Football history was being unfolded and retold for the benefit of just Dad and I, by the man closest to the events.

This was a post-match analysis of the very highest order. Pure magic. Dad was open-mouthed throughout, while I sat bolt upright, hanging on Sir Geoff's every word. Dad recalled how he had watched the game on a black and white TV set back in Haverfordwest. Being only two years old in 1966, I had no recollection of the famous final. Sir Geoff though, had described the events in such rich terms, that I felt that I had now enjoyed the match with my father. It was a special moment that I shall never forget, cementing the bond between father and son.

Thanks, Geoff.

Sir Geoff very kindly signed his autobiography, personalised for me as we sat in my office. We laughed together as I recounted how I had once queued outside a wet Ninian Park for his signature following a game between Cardiff City and Chelsea, during his spell as manager of the Stamford Bridge outfit. He had signed with good grace for that teenage autograph hunter back then.

During our spell of working together, Sir Geoff told me how he had accepted a role with an overseas company, along similar lines to his role with JPA. This time his partners would be Olympian Sir Steven Redgrave and England Rugby World Cup star Tony Underwood. The famous trio would invest in the Royal Marbella Group, Spanish property developers.

Sir Geoff asked if I was also interested in investing in a property with him in Spain with the Royal Marbella Group. I stumped up the cash, confident that a second business association with Sir Geoff, could only be a force for good. Initially, it sounded like an attractive and viable scheme, supported by some high-end backers.

Unfortunately, the venture did not end well, culminating in a £2 million High Court claim for money lost when the proposed luxury apartments in Marbella were never built. Some investors lost their deposits when schemes were scrapped. The trio of sporting superstars maintained that, while some projects were completed, others, including Lince Sanctuario near Seville, where Redgrave had reportedly invested £2 million in an off-plan villa, would never see the light of day. Fortunately, none of my own firm's clients had been persuaded to invest in the scheme.

I decided not to become part of the potentially expensive legal challenge, which had no real guarantee of success anyway, our lawyers advised. Neither Redgrave nor Underwood were among the claimants in the High Court action either. I decided to take the hit and absorb the significant six-figure financial loss which I had incurred. My accountants and professional advisors explained that the bigger picture should usually outrank any emotional involvement. Wise words.

World Cup heroes of the round and oval ball? Knighted Olympic legends? Had I, for once, been starstruck by such names? Perhaps. Though in hindsight, I cannot help recollecting my slight unease when meeting up with representatives of the development company. I don't know, it just somehow didn't quite feel right really. I should have listened to myself.

I did not hold Sir Geoff responsible for any of these events of course. We had both acted in good faith, sensing a genuine business opportunity and both ended up in disappointment, not to mention out of pocket. He later told me that he wished that he had invested in Grosvenor Waterside Chelsea instead, whose properties my organisation had promoted with great results for our clients who had invested there.

Sir Geoff and I maintained our business relationship and I was proud that he continued as a non-executive director. Towards the end of my sporting career, he also attended functions to launch my enterprise Power Goldberg in London and Cardiff.

Power Goldberg brought together a team of professionals with a wealth of experience in all areas of sports and entertainment management. Our service was fully inclusive and covered contract negotiation and transfers but also other areas such as expert financial advice, retirement planning, PR, marketing, and legal & property services.

I recall my days with Sir Geoff Hurst MBE with nothing but pride, happiness, and a great deal of friendship.

I dealt with the Marbella episode and learned some harsh lessons from the bittersweet experience. My own property portfolio of central London properties was doing well enough for me to absorb the Spanish loss. I suppose I realised then though that, despite my successful career to date and some decisions which had stood me in good stead, not every plan would succeed.

Remember this if you are intent on climbing the ladder to success. Not every horse you back will romp to victory.

Think with your head, not your heart.

Sir Bob

With the success we were enjoying with Sir Geoff Hurst on board as a patron, it never really occurred to me to bring in another non-executive director or patron. After all, who else was there who was of the same stature and standing in the world of sport as Sir Geoff?

I was in a client meeting at my 'office' in Selfridges Hotel one day with Mick Wandsworth, the Barnsley-born football coach and former player. Mick's colourful journey around the football globe, had seen him enjoy spells as manager of Frickley Athletic, Matlock Town, Huddersfield Town, Portuguese outfit Beira-Mar, and even the Democratic Republic of Congo national side. He was a great supporter of ours and often made referrals to my company.

During the discussion, Mick had been flicking through my company brochure. His eye was caught by the endorsement from

Sir Geoff Hurst.

Mick had a very dry sense of humour. He was a typical Yorkshireman. I always thoroughly enjoyed my meetings with him, even if it was occasionally hard to tell whether he was being serious.

He was a real football man though, and his varied career had included a spell as Assistant Manager to Sir Bobby Robson at Newcastle United. He had also held down a role between 1988 and 1992 as an official match observer for the England national team under both Bobby Robson and Graham Taylor. In earlier times he had been an FA regional coach in the northwest region of England. His coaching CV included some impressive work with the Football Association.

During our meeting, Mick announced that he had a contact he felt I should meet. He believed that JPA could benefit from another patron, alongside Sir Geoff. The next thing I knew, he was on his phone. "Hi boss, it's Mick......"

Mick explained to his "boss" that he was ringing from a business meeting with his professional adviser who was achieving some decent results on behalf of clients from the worlds of sports and entertainment. He referenced the fact that Sir Geoff had accepted a role with the enterprise. This was enough to attract interest from Mick's "boss." The phone passed to me.

Familiar Geordie tones greeted me. "It's Bobby Robson here. How are you lad?"

In momentary shock, I managed to compose myself from the other end of the phone. I needed to retain my professionalism here. I would not get a second chance to create a first impression, as they say.

Sir Bobby Robson CBE was, quite simply, a football icon. A figure adored on Tyneside, his achievements in the game had made him a national treasure. A successful spell at the humble Suffolk club Ipswich Town had seen him collect the FA Cup in 1978 and UEFA Cup in 1981. A stint in the England hot seat followed as he led the Three Lions to the 1986 World Cup in Mexico ("It wasn't the hand of God; it was the hand of a rascal."

Sir Bob declared.)

His place in the nation's hearts was probably secured though, during Italia 90. Gazza's tears, an agonising penalty defeat. A 'world in motion' watched as the England football community followed every kick over those long, hot, summer nights. "Nessun Dorma".

Gary Lineker, England goalscoring hero said that he had never played for a more enthusiastic man than Bobby Robson. Terry Butcher, Sir Bobby's skipper in that famous Turin clash with West Germany has described how Robson would always accentuate positives. He felt like he could run through a brick wall for the boss.

Robson went on to manage a host of significant continental clubs after that: PSV Eindhoven, Porto, and Barcelona. Cups and titles at all. He was declared European Manager of the Year for 1996–97.

Inevitably, perhaps, his final managerial post had seen him take charge at Newcastle United, the club he had supported as a boy. Robson assumed the reins at St James' Park in 1999 and guided the club to European qualification on several occasions. Despite ultimately losing his post in 2004, Bobby Robson retains the affections of the Geordie nation. He received the freedom of Newcastle upon Tyne the following year. There is a Bobby Robson statue at St James' Park. He was also a Freeman of Durham and Ipswich.

In 2002 a statue of Sir Bobby was unveiled at the home of Ipswich Town, in honour of the great man's achievements in charge at Portman Road. He accepted the role of honorary president at Ipswich in 2006 until his death from lung cancer in 2009. He received the CBE in 1991 for services to football and was knighted in 2002.

In 2013, as part of the 150th-anniversary celebrations of the FA, the FA designated the 10th of August as Sir Bobby Robson National Football Day.

You can read tributes about the power, humility, and sheer warmth of this man from giants of the international football world. Beckenbauer (Germany), Shearer (England), Raul (Spain), Luis Figo (Portugal), and even Brazilian superstar, Ronaldo. He was held in high regard by such figures. The motto of the biggest club he managed; Barcelona is "Més que un club." "More than a club." 2018 saw the release of a film dedicated to this much-loved son of a Durham miner: "Bobby Robson: More than a Manager."

I explained the nature of our organisation to Sir Bobby, who was especially taken by the role played by Sir Geoff Hurst. The conversation took place not long after Sir Bobby had left his position at The Toon. He offered to take soundings from Sir Geoff before discussing a potential way forward for him and me to work together if that is what I wanted to happen.

I indicated that I was prepared to agree to this suggestion.

In truth, I was over the moon, but you must maintain your composure in the business world, especially in this kind of company.

Mick passed over my contact details and Sir Bobby Robson would be in touch.

I may have quietly pinched myself.

True to his word, the former England manager, who also shared my love of cricket incidentally, subsequently called, and arranged for us to meet when he was next in the capital. He kept a house in Fulham. (Robson made 152 appearances as a player for Fulham in the 50s and managed the West London outfit briefly in 1968, a side which had included a young Malcolm Macdonald.)

Sir Bobby and I arranged to meet at a breakfast meeting to be held in a Kensington hotel. I was looking forward immensely to meeting a figure of his stature. I may even have been a little nervous if truth be told, though it would be important to keep a lid on that.

Sir Bobby was accompanied at the breakfast table by his lawyer, Peter Millichip, son of Sir Bert Millichip, who had served as chairman of the Football Association during some tough times for the game in England.

The Heysel Stadium disaster, the Bradford City stadium fire, and the Hillsborough disaster had all taken place during his chairmanship. Peter was a big West Bromwich Albion fan and a close friend of Sir Bobby.

I worked hard to sell myself during what turned out to be a successful meeting. Sir Bobby was very enthusiastic. He noticed that my publicity brochure included a reference to Craig Bellamy, amidst many other sports stars. Craig had played for Sir Bob at Newcastle United. Bellars had been a great player, he advised, if a little hard to manage! Sir Bobby told a great story of how he had tried to sign the Welshman earlier in his career, but the Cardiff Kiddie decided to join Gordon Strachan at Coventry City. Sir Bobby laughed when he discovered that I had in fact, driven Craig Bellamy to Coventry City for him to conclude the transfer negotiations. For his part, Craig described Robson as "the best manager I have ever worked with."

The meeting concluded with terms agreed. Sir Bobby confirmed that he would become a patron of my organisation. I was overjoyed.

There was just something special about Sir Bobby Robson. Sure, his record of achievements in the game was impressive but there was more to it than that. Much more. There was simply an aura around this figure of sporting royalty. Sir Bobby became a special person in my life and I miss him deeply. I recall our times together with great affection.

One of our meetings took place in the same venue that the England Cricket Team was also using. Famous faces from the cricketing world had noticed us. Freddie Flintoff and others. At the conclusion of our exchange, they formed an orderly queue to meet up with Sir Bobby!

I felt privileged to have two legendary figures such as the two Sirs on board. I also knew the commercial value that would be added to my enterprise by their names as Sir Bobby fulfilled his role in a similar way to Sir Geoff Hurst, helping with PR and speaking to potential clients. It was all a great demonstration of just how far I had come and the world that our small team now inhabited. I was enormously proud of our success.

A business evening was held one night at Stamford Bridge,

the home of Chelsea FC. Many of our football business clients were in attendance along with figures from the wider sporting community and stars of the entertainment world. The event would introduce Sir Bobby and my organisation, promoting a property development opportunity with special terms to my clients.

I made sure that all my staff was present at the event. We were a family, and it was important to me that they felt fully part of the set-up. They had met Sir Geoff and Sir Bobby was just as special to us. We ended the evening in a London nightspot, where our celebrations continued into the small hours. Sir Bobby did not party with us until dawn though as he was due to fly out to attend a match the following day.

As Sir Bobby had stood on the front of the stage at the home of Chelsea FC, outlining his role and endorsing me to our invited audience, I bristled with pride from the wings. It was one of the proudest moments of my life.

Here I was, at a prestigious London venue with a national treasure extolling my virtues to an invited, celebrity audience. At times it felt like one of those *Audience With...* television shows produced by London Weekend Television in which a famous host, usually a singer or comedian, performs for an invited audience of celebrity guests, interspersed with questions from the audience, in a light-hearted revue/tribute style. *An Audience with Jonathan Power?*

It was hard to fully appreciate just how far I had travelled since I first clattered around the streets of Cardiff delivering telegram greetings by pushbike.

I recalled the lack of confidence shown in me by teachers like Mr Brain, the absence of any motivation imparted to me by my superiors at BT and yes, I heard again the words of Kathy Mackay's mother from that Belfast showdown.

"I would amount to nothing; I could never provide for her Kathy. Kathy would be better off without me."

I wish they could all have been in the crowd at Chelsea that night.

Growing up. L-R Colin, Dad, David, Maggie, Mum and me.

Andy Cole with Sir Alex Ferguson

With Ian Wright

With John Fashanu and Joe Calzaghe as we expanded into new
office premises

It was a privilege to have Sir Geoff Hurst
on board as Non-Executive Director

Sir Geoff Hurst and Bob the Drunk share a laugh
on the set of 'Kicking Off'

Honoured to have had Sir Bobby Robson as the patron of my organisation

With Mike Tyson and Joe Calzaghe

Famous clients from The Jonathan Power Associates brochure

With Mike Love of the Beach Boys, Legal and General
Conference, Hong Kong, 1994

At the Apollo Theatre, making my West End debut as a Producer

With Idina Menzel

Welcoming Sir Tim Rice at the Idina Menzel opening night

With Nigel Lythgoe at the LA opening of Snow White

With Sir Ian McKellen and theatre producer
Karen Struel-White, discussing upcoming projects

As Captain Williams in the feature film 'Allies'

With Matt and Emma Willis at the premier of 'Allies'

Starring alongside Togo Igawa in the film 'Chameleon'

With Emeli Sande at Elton John's Aids Foundation Party

With Lionel Richie

With Ollie Alexander

With Nile Rogers

Millie Power with Ed Sheeran backstage at the Royal Variety Performance

With my wife Emma and daughter Millie

The JP International XI

As you will have seen, I have been lucky enough to work with many top international stars from the football world down the years.

It hasn't all been down to good fortune of course, as hard work, a 24/7 schedule and a certain degree of business acumen all played their part. Business relationships do not simply drop out of the sky.

At times though, yes, I suppose that Lady Luck has dealt me a decent hand. My endeavours have been rewarded with the trappings of success. Seats at the best tables, tickets for the biggest matches and an eye-watering collection of famous names in my phone book. My walls were adorned with signed memorabilia. So many players donated signed items as a "thank you" for our services. The walls of our two-storey office attracted many an admiring glance from our clients.

In contemplating the idea for this book, many of the top football players I have worked with sprang readily to mind. Household names from the screens of Sky and BT. International superstars. World Cup legends.

I once casually imagined them all in the same dressing room, the same team even.

How would that look, I wondered?

Oh no. I had gone and done it now. The genie was out of the bottle. There would be no turning back from this task; my three wishes would centre on defence, midfield and attack.

This could take some time, I thought.

I decided to arrange my stars in an unimaginative 4-3-3 formation. To be honest, though, I reassured myself that this set-up would be a less than rigid structure as some of these guys, as you will see, were certainly no strangers to the art of doing their own thing. I would look for leaders, flair, charisma, and star quality in my imaginary dressing room.

The only selection criteria would be that, at some point in

their adventures, each one of them would have to have been a business associate of mine somewhere along the line. Genuine partnership arrangements, not simply a "Sign 'ere Mister?" would get you into this dressing room. Invitation only.

Many of my clients came by referral and recommendation. Sometimes the contact continued via agents though often it was through direct contact with the players themselves. I didn't advertise. I didn't need to. We had a great reputation led by two Sirs. My company brochure was my business card, endorsed by the great names of Sir Geoff Hurst and Sir Bobby Robson.

The short biography of each player shows the strength of their achievements and the calibre of the international stars I advised. I had some great times with so many of these guys over the years. Many of the stories of our times together feature throughout the pages of this book. I was an advisor, friend, and confidant.

Welcome to JP's team of All-Stars.
I began in goal.

GOALKEEPER

I advised many admirable goalkeepers down the years. From my early days working with the likes of Seamus Kelly who played a handful of games at Cardiff City, through to encountering those who guarded the woodwork at some of the top Premier League outfits.

Keepers like Paul Gerrard of Everton, Paul Rachubka, who spent time at Old Trafford. Welsh international Martyn Margetson of Manchester City and later the England coaching set-up. A young Joe Hart became a client while learning his trade at Shrewsbury Town. He was destined for great things even then, head and shoulders above the rest.

For my No.1 choice between the sticks though, I am going for a real giant of the modern game.

David James

Welwyn Garden City-born David James could probably only have played in the era that he did. He is most definitely a man of his time. That exotic film star looks, Amazonian physique and experimental hairstyles were simply a gift to ad men.

His modelling talents were put to good use by Giorgio Armani in 1995 and H&M in 2005. He had first risen to fame with Liverpool teammates Steve McManaman, Jamie Redknapp, and Robbie Fowler, who were nicknamed the Spice Boys, a reference to the quintessential 90s girl power giants the Spice Girls. Who could forget those 1996 Cup Final white suits?

There is more to James than Panini stickers, appearances on *Strictly Come Dancing* or advertising designer label clothing though. Much more.

James played for the top clubs. Villa, Liverpool, Manchester City. An FA Cup winner with Pompey. League Cup success at Anfield.

He is fourth on the list of all-time Premier League appearances, having played in 572 top-level matches, and held the Premier League record for most clean sheets with 169 until Petr Čech overcame the record. The only names above him on that list of PL greats are Gareth Barry, Ryan Giggs and Frank Lampard. It's a decent company I am sure you would agree. 53 England caps have adorned that well-coiffured barnet too by the way.

DEFENCE

This was a tough call.

I made some great 'signings' over the years. From international names to stalwarts of the lower divisions. A quick glance through the names of some of the guys who failed to make it into my All-Star XI will give some impression of the cosmopolitan defenders on our books:

Darren Moore is one of the most respected men in the game. Northern Ireland international Gareth McCauley is described by former England boss Roy Hodgson as his best-ever signing.

Jamie Lawrence, former Leicester City star and Jamaican international.

Frank Sinclair has 28 caps for Jamaica and 650 appearances for the likes of Chelsea, Leicester City and Burnley.

Robert Page, who played with distinction for Watford and later managed the Wales international side.

Steve Staunton: over 480 appearances with Liverpool, Villa and others and the first man to earn 100 international caps for the Republic of Ireland.

Jason Van Blerk, whose CV includes spells in Belgium, the Netherlands and Australia. 27 full caps for the Socceroo star from Sydney.

Alan Stubbs. The former Everton man won all three domestic trophies in Scotland during a successful spell north of the border with Celtic.

There are many other names I could have recounted here but the ones who finally made it into my dressing room, underline the international nature of our client base. Very top names from the very top of the game.

Of course, if we are also talking top defensive tactics, then we must talk Italian.

Alessandro Pistone

The Milanese full back starred for Internazionale alongside Gianluca Festa, Paul Ince, and Benito Carbone. With 45 Serie A appearances for I Nerazzurri, Alessandro became a mainstay in defence and played a significant part in their march to the 1997 UEFA Cup Final, where they were defeated on penalties by the German outfit FC Schalke 04.

Kenny Dalglish paid £4.5 million to take the stylish left back to Newcastle United before a subsequent spell at Everton was hit by injury, though he still turned out over 100 times for the Toffees. He also endured a colourful dust-up with big Duncan Ferguson whilst at Goodison!

Pistone was part of the victorious Italian side that won the European Under-21 Championships in 1996 and earned Olympic recognition for the Azzurri at Atlanta in 1996.

A keen poker player, Pistone could be a surprise trump card in my star-studded selection.

Some critics of Pistone may have felt that despite his qualities, he may have been slightly lacking in some of the more 'robust' qualities required to truly succeed in the English game. To complement this, I have therefore added some 'steel' to sit alongside the cultured Italian. A couple of proper, tough-as-teak defensive linchpins.

John Terry

Cast your mind back to the opening pages of this book. Remember? We looked at how some top sports stars are known by a single name, or even just by their initials.

John Terry is known throughout football circles as simply, JT. He has become the very definition of the word 'centre half,' plugging gaps in the Chelsea defence and chipping in with a clutch of goals. He has set the standards for others – Harry Maguire for instance – to follow as the model stopper. A talisman of the modern Premier League, JT would probably have been a success in any era. It is not hard to imagine him lining up alongside Chopper Harris in front of the Chelsea Shed or even doing the ugly work in front of the silky skills of Bobby Moore in 1966.

Although best known for his bravery, leadership and aggressive tackling, the Stamford Bridge legend was also an intelligent player, with a keen positional awareness and an ability to read the game. This compensated for any perceived absence of mobility or athleticism. Let us not forget 40-plus goals for The Blues either. He even once played in goal, keeping a clean sheet against Reading.

JT's attributes brought extensive international reward and recognition: 78 England caps plus a host of honours in the club game; five Premier League titles, five FA Cups, three League Cups, one UEFA Champions League and one UEFA Europa League. His individual honours include being featured in the all-star squad for the 2006 FIFA World Cup, the only English player to make the selection.

John Terry is, quite simply, part of Premier League history.

Rio Ferdinand

I know that this international line-up is something of a fantasy exercise but it has been a revelation, even to myself, in highlighting the quality of names we handled during some stellar careers.

Also though, I want it to be a proper team. I have thought about formations and how each of its famous components might fit together. After all, as the late former Liverpool boss Bill Shankly once said, "a football team is like a piano. You need eight men to carry it and three who can play the damn thing."

Despite his obvious defensive prowess, JT was often paired with a mobile ball-playing centre-back, such as Ricardo Carvalho at Chelsea or Rio Ferdinand for England. I like the sound of combining two of my higher-end clients like this in my dream team.

Ferdinand won 81 full caps for England in a glittering career with, principally, West Ham United, Leeds United and, most notably, Manchester United. If anything, his trophy cabinet is even more impressive than Terry's, with medals in the major club tournaments, including the 2008 FIFA Club World Cup.

Rio epitomised the modern defender, with his balance, control and composure.

Ben Iroha

Legendary Brazilian Pele once famously predicted that an African nation would win the World Cup by the year 2000.

Although this prediction was found to be somewhat short of

the mark, there is no doubt that the nations from across the huge continent have made a significant contribution to the world game.

Nigeria's record is decent on the world stage, having reached the last 16 of the World Cup in 1994, 1998 and 2014. Olympic gold medallists in 1996. The Super Eagles have also produced some decent individual players.

One of my favourite clients, Ben Iroha, was a versatile defender who helped establish Nigeria on the global stage during the 1990s. His club career took saw him play in Nigeria, Spain, the USA, and England – with Watford. He was a contemporary of Jay-Jay Okocha. He appeared at the World Cup in 1994 and 1998 and starred when the Super Eagles triumphed in the 1994 Africa Nations Cup. The full-back or midfielder won 50 caps for Nigeria between 1990 and 1998. It was a treat to work with him.

MIDFIELD

Well, I am reasonably satisfied with that for my cosmopolitan back four. A nice blend of strength and subtlety, I think.

Moving up the field, I again found myself overlooking some household names from my international client base. Robbie Savage will no doubt be on the blower as soon as the Welsh international discovers that he did not make the cut, while Turkish ace Muzzy Izzet was a force for Leicester City alongside Sav back in the day, winning silverware together in the 2000 Worthington Cup Final against Tranmere Rovers. Matt Jones was another Leicester City old boy that didn't make the cut – another Welsh international.

Salif Diao played for Liverpool from 2002 to 2007 and played international football for Senegal.

Only three could occupy the centre stage for me though. Here are my choices.

Michael Carrick

With over 300 games for Manchester United, Michael Carrick is more than capable of "carrying the piano" for the JPXI.

One of the most decorated players in the English game, the 34-times capped holding midfielder captained the Old Trafford club. He won every domestic honour in the English game.

Sometimes the sort of player to go under the radar, Carrick's admirers nevertheless came from the very top of the game. Indeed, Pep Guardiola described him as "one of the best holding midfielders I've ever seen." Pep compared the Wallsend Boys' Club product favourably, alongside Barcelona's Xabi Alonso and Sergio Busquets of Bayern Munich.

I think we can trust Pep's judgement, don't you?

Joe Cole

Some critics argue that Joe Cole failed to fully deliver on his potential across a wide career, or that injuries held him back. I am not so sure.

Joe spent seven seasons at Stamford Bridge, winning all the major domestic honours. He appeared alongside Terry in the 2007/08 Champions League Final defeat to Manchester United on a night when Rio Ferdinand and Michael Carrick lined up for the victorious Red Devils in Moscow.

The popular Londoner played over 700 games for West Ham, Chelsea, Liverpool, Lille (France), Aston Villa, Coventry City and Florida's Tampa Bay Rowdies in a career which included 56 full England caps. He was selected alongside Terry for the PFA Team of the Year in 2006. One of my proudest possessions is a shirt they both signed for me in the players' lounge after a Chelsea match, which I attended at Stamford Bridge.

Joe's other individual honours include Player of the Year at Chelsea in 2008 and West Ham's Hammer of the Year in 2003. Indeed, he always struck me as a 'fan's player.' The kind of player that the guy in the stands thinks of as 'one of our own.'

In a statement published to herald his retirement in 2018, he said, "As a fan, I loved watching wholehearted, skilful players and this is what inspired me. I remembered what was special for me when I was sitting in the stands watching games and I tried to replicate this. I hope I was able to do this for some of the fans and people who have watched my games over the years."

In the multimillion-pound world of modern professional football, these are sentiments which will resonate with many an ordinary fan. Nice one Joe.

Craig Bellamy

Craig is one of those guys who divides opinion. He wore his heart on his sleeve and played with passion and intensity. Woe betide you if you failed to come up to his standards on the field of play.

This was a man opposition fans loved to hate, yet he earned the love of supporters at some of the biggest clubs around, Liverpool, Celtic, and Newcastle United. He remains especially loved in his hometown of Cardiff for the role he played in finally bringing Premier League action to the Bluebirds. Anfield legend Steve Gerrard has paid tribute to his professionalism. Mark Hughes talks about the Welshman's desire to affect every game he plays.

Moreover, Craig Bellamy was simply an exceptionally great player.

Craig earned 78 caps for Wales, including a goalscoring performance in a memorable victory over Italy in 2002. He scored goals wherever he played, and his all-action style made him a threat to anyone on his day. I'm giving Bellars a free role in my 4-3-3 line-up because of his achievements.... and he's from Cardiff!

ATTACK

If the pool of players from which I have already drawn gave me

121

some selection headaches, it is up front that I encountered even tougher choices.

My striking clients spanned the whole football world. Names to add the 'fire power' to the Power XI, you might say.

Guys like Yakubu, the 57-times capped Nigerian Olympian who played in England, Israel, China and Turkey; Stern John, scorer of over 70 international goals for Trinidad & Tobago; and Michel Ngonge, whose career took him to Belgium, Turkey, England and Scotland, with international recognition for Zaire/Democratic Republic of Congo.

Despite this hatful of riches from across the globe though, I have gone for three homegrown stars to grab the goals in my dream line-up. These three certainly knew how to stick the chances away. I think they might just have been powerful forces in the dressing room too.

Andrew Cole

Andrew Cole is seen as something of a quiet man at times.

Put him anywhere the goal though and it was all over bar the shouting.

Signed by Alex Ferguson for Manchester United from Newcastle United in 1995 for a record fee, Cole went on to lift several Premier League titles at Old Trafford, plus the Champions League and three FA Cups. Cole helped United to the historic treble in 1999. His partnership with Dwight Yorke set pulses raising across Europe in dazzling displays. Cole is synonymous with the 'Glory, Glory' days of the modern Manchester United. His subsequent League Cup triumph with Blackburn Rovers completed an impressive collection of medals.

Another top striker whose prowess in front of goal never quite gained the international recognition they perhaps earned, Cole's goalscoring record at his peak was phenomenal. His contribution to the team is also not to be ignored, as he was the first footballer to finish on top of the Premier League's goalscoring charts *and* assist charts in the same season.

Like others in my dream team, Cole has also done his bit for others. Following a trip to Zimbabwe, Cole established his own charitable foundation – the Andy Cole Children's Foundation, to help AIDS orphans there. He also set up the Andy Cole Fund to raise money for Kidney Research UK, after his own well-publicised kidney problems.

Ian Wright

Wrighty.
     Where to even start eh?
     If we start with the basic stats, Ian Wright turned out with success for Palace and Arsenal while he also enjoyed stints at West Ham and Celtic, amongst others.
     Silverware was amassed at Highbury, but it is his goalscoring record for which he is most remembered, topping the list of Gunners' Goalscoring Greats until surpassed by Thierry Henri.
     Wrighty played and sometimes lived on the edge. Passion, speed, aggression. It's not hard to imagine him on the North Bank, Highbury or in the Holmesdale Road Stand at Selhurst Park if he hadn't been playing – yelling and screaming with the rest of the home fans.
     His 33 England caps are a small reward for his feats though and he was often overlooked when it came to the big international moments.
     Wrighty's media career would take almost as long to reference as his work on the football field.
     Top of the Pops, Top Gear, Match of the Day, Friday Night's All Wright, I'm a Celebrity. He has advertised 'Chicken Tonight' and recorded a pop record called, inevitably, "Do the Right Thing". A children's author and social commentator, he is an example of a celebrity whose success comes from being, simply himself. He is hugely popular as a pundit and wears his heart on his sleeve, just like when he played.
     His personality is his popularity. It's hard not to love him. After all, 1.9m Twitter followers can't be wrong.

John Fashanu

I have left Fash until last. Deliberately.

My side is full of big characters and larger-than-life dressing room leaders but, well, Fash is simply a league apart.

Part of the original Wimbledon Crazy Gang of the late 80s, Fash took the word 'intimidating' to new levels. A black belt in karate, defenders knew just what to expect from Fash the Bash ….and they usually got it.

A quick resumé of his life might take in the fact that he was a Barnardo's boy who grew up to play for Wimbledon in its FA Cup winning pomp and was capped twice for England too; then there was his co-presenting of the television phenomenon *Gladiators*, alongside Ulrika Jonsson and an ambassadorial role with the Federal Republic of Nigeria.

Fash was a gladiator in more ways than one. With a career total of 149 goals you get the impression that Fash got the better of some opponents before a ball was even kicked. His enormous physique, kill-or-be-killed attitude and dominating presence epitomised the Wimbledon way. In a team of notorious hard men, Fash was top dog. A pit bull in a bear pit. Games were there to be won. Whatever it took. I dare not leave him out.

The full line-up then is as follows:

David James

Alessandro Pistone   John Terry   Rio Ferdinand   Ben Iroha

Michael Carrick   Joe Cole

Craig Bellamy

Andrew Cole   Ian Wright   John Fashanu

124

Manager? Well, it just had to be…Sir Bobby Robson CBE.

What a cracking line up eh? Representation from across the globe. I am going to hand the skipper's armband to JT. A natural leader who might just be able to keep Bellamy, Wright and Fash in check.

I wonder how much my team would all be worth in today's transfer market…

A World of Sport

Not all clients came from the world of football. Our stable included names from across the sporting fraternity.

The oval ball also provided plenty of business for example. I recall being introduced to Simon Geoghegan, the 37-times-capped Irish rugby union winger who starred for London Irish and Bath in their heyday. Bath had been particularly successful in the 80s and 90s and was the first English side to win the European Cup in 1998.

Simon and I got on famously. We would socialise a great deal and he became a great friend as well as a client. When his playing days were over, he became a partner in the London law firm Roslin King. Simon was so impressed by the service he received from us that he went on to refer many of the Bath Rugby stars to us.

That referral word-of-mouth process produced results for me more than times I care to remember. We may have sponsored the odd event or publication here and there, but I didn't have an advertising budget to speak of; there was simply no need for one. Our track record was our marketing strategy. The guys on *Dragon's Den* would never have gone for it but show me a cost code allocation with the heading 'hard work' and then we'll talk. Results simply fed results. My address book would show evidence of that. That was the only audit trail I needed.

Don't get me wrong. Our business was underpinned by rigid compliance checks and quality assurance processes. Every scrap of financial advice was backed up by stringent tests to ensure that it best suited the needs of our elite clients. You simply don't advise British Lions and Grand Slam winners off the back of a fag packet.

The secret of our success though was the referrals made on our behalf by the guys we advised. It is hard to quantify but leading Bath names such as winger Adedayo Adebayo, full-back Matt Perry, prop forward Victor Ubogu, multi-talented Mike

Catt, Ian Balshaw, the towering Steve Ojomoh and hooker Lee Mears all came to us because of our reputation.

Mark Regan was another client who played for Bath, England and the British Lions.

Our clients also included South African star Hentie Martens and, keeping the Welsh flag flying, Gareth Cooper. These two were battling out for the scrum half position at the Memorial Ground, Bath at the time. It was a great time to be associated with the success of the West country outfit, which could justifiably claim to have been one of the most successful UK sporting institutions of the day.

Wales and England internationals, British and Irish Lions, backs, forwards, stars of the Southern Hemisphere. At one game I attended I think I counted ten of our clients in the starting line-up.

Other rugby stars came our way. Wales prop Martyn Madden (all 19 stones of him!) and father and son duo Paul and Jamie Ringer – both capped for Wales – for example.

Ringer Sr. was born in Leeds but represented Wales at both Union and League codes. He will always be remembered for receiving his marching orders against England at Twickenham in the red jersey of Wales in a famous clash between these old rivals back in 1980. He was sent off for a late challenge on English outside half John Horton (another Bath man) and, perhaps consequently, did not make the Lions squad tour South Africa later that year.

The abrasive forward may have been at home against the Springboks though, where injuries against the tough Southern Hemisphere opponents played a part in the Lions going down to defeat against uncompromising hosts. South Africa won the series 3-1 against the tourists who were badly hit by injuries. Wisely, I never saw fit to remind the fiery flanker of that Twickers dismissal!

Other clients came from the more hushed surroundings of the snooker room.

Robbie Savage called me to say that he would like me to

meet his friend, the snooker player Mark Williams. That referral from Sav brought Mark Williams and Stephen Hendry to us via their agent Lee Doyle, chairman of Stirling-based 110 Sports Group.

Welshman Williams had been the first left-handed player to become World Champion and lifted the crown on three occasions. Scottish-born Hendry had simply been one of the game's most accomplished performers and had dominated the sport during the 90s, winning the World Championship seven times. Little wonder that he earned the nickname The King of the Crucible, such was his domination of the annual World Championship tournament held at the Crucible Theatre, Sheffield.

Hendry is one of the all-time greats of the green baize. It was a great thrill to hook up with him through my business connections. Wheels within wheels.

We also played a round of golf at times.

Glaswegian Alastair Forsyth was a client when associated with 110 Sports Management. After a promising amateur career, he turned professional in 1998 and played on the European Tour for several years, acquitting himself well on behalf of Scottish golf. Rangers fan Forsyth's name was certainly up there alongside the golfing great and good in the new millennium.

One of my Independent Financial Advisers, Robbie Weston advised athletes Matt Elias and Olympian Iwan Thomas. Thomas himself is a former European, Commonwealth Games and World Champion. We also worked with six-times Olympian, the effervescent, larger-than-life, Tessa Sanderson. Jamaican-born Tessa was the first black British woman to win an Olympic gold medal.

Sanderson enjoyed an astonishing career. She once threw a javelin 73 metres and also ran 400 metres in less than a minute. Her success includes gold medals in the javelin at three Commonwealth Games and success at the 1992 IAAF World Cup. Her achievements span the UK, European and Commonwealth stages. Her career has been recognised by the awarding of an MBE, OBE, and CBE.

We also provided advice to the Olympic couple Diane and Vicente Modhal.

Diane ran with grace and style over 800 metres, achieving success at the Commonwealth Games level and various international competitions. Impressively, she represented Great Britain at no less than four Olympic Games (1988–2000), reaching an Olympic final in 1988. Her husband Vicente was a Norwegian international athletics coach and footballer's agent.

Sprinter Jamie Baulch was a particular ambassador for us and a guy to whom I easily warmed. A lively character, Jamie had been born in Nottingham, but raised by adoptive parents in Risca, near Newport, South Wales. He had to work hard to succeed in a sport considered in some quarters to be middle-class.

Jamie worked in my organisation in a business development capacity and was instrumental when we even set up a free 'concierge' type service for clients both old and new. We would help organise holidays, obtain discounts from high-end clothing suppliers, arrange entry to top London nightspots and open a variety of other commercial doors. This was typical of the 'added value' service we provided. Going the extra mile to not only meet but exceed our client's expectations.

Jamie's athletics career includes indoor titles, a silver medal at the 1996 Olympics and silver and bronze Commonwealth Games representing his adopted Wales.

Jamie formed part of the British 4 × 400m relay team which finished second in the 1997 World Championships. However, in 2010 it was announced that the British team were to be awarded the gold medal as they were beaten by a United States team which included Antonio Pettigrew, who had confessed to taking performance-enhancing drugs, thus disqualifying the US team. Baulch received his World Championship gold medal in May 2010. Despite his pride, he admitted: "It would have been great to have been in front of 80,000 people up on the rostrum. Nothing can replace that. This is a second-best, unfortunately, but it's nice to be recognised."

In retirement, Baulch established several businesses, such as

Definitive, a sports management company and sports memorabilia company Authentic Sports. He became an ambassador for the Jaguar Academy of Sport where he played an important role in bringing forward future sporting talent.

Along with Savage, Bellamy, and Power, Baulch is a fiercely proud Welshman.

I liked Jamie. We shared much common ground. He had won his first national title aged around 15 years old at Cwmbran Stadium in Torfaen, Gwent, just outside Newport. A stadium which once staged the first ever Champions League tie in Wales.

Reflecting on his humble origins, Jamie has commented on how anybody with aspirations must just start somewhere. It's the journey and the lessons we learn along the way that are important, he opines. Persistence, consistency and enjoying what we do is the key. "Never give up as you don't know where you will end up."

Wise words mate.

Cricket has always been near to my heart. I love everything about it. The chess-board strategy of the five-day test; the 'play in a day' drama of the one-day game or the 'TV dinner' 20/20 version. I have been lucky enough to travel the world following Test cricket – and before Paul Ringer hauls me over the coals for supporting the Old Enemy, it's the England and Wales Cricket Board by the way!

Glamorgan offspinner Robert Croft has likened playing for Glamorgan to representing Wales, and playing for England to like playing for the Lions!

Since 1997, the England and Wales Cricket Board have governed the England set-up.

As a South Wales lad, I was especially pleased to be able to advise Steve Watkin who played with distinction for Glamorgan and England. Welsh-born players can represent England in cricket as, as I say, the England cricket team represents England and Wales in the international game. Maesteg seamer Watkin took a career total of 902 wickets.

He had been granted a testimonial season by Glamorgan

County Cricket Club as a loyalty reward for playing for the county for 10 years. The funds raised during that season's campaign also attracted tax benefits. This made a significant difference to the cricketer's earnings, so my advice and services were sought by Steve. This was all before cricketers played in the riches of the Indian Premier League, where a top-rated player can earn a million pounds for a few weeks' work, and test team players of today earning lucrative central contract salaries. Cricket players used to earn modest salaries in comparison.

When I was advising, typically, a county cricket player would get paid by the county they played for during the cricket season which would run from April to September. The player would then have to get a 'normal job' for the autumn and winter months. How things have changed. Steve's test career included a "5-for" against the West Indies at Headingley; a certain Viv Richards is one of his victims. Maybe Steve was born too soon?

Boxing also gave us some fun.

You will have read earlier that my company advised Joe Calzaghe for several years.

I also enjoyed a special relationship with one of Wales's favourite sporting sons, former World Featherweight Champion Steve Robinson and sponsored some of the equipment brought in to support a new fitness centre he was setting up. We had been advising him for some time and it was great to retain the relationship as he set out on a new course.

One of the boxing stars we advised was a particular character.

Battersea Bomber Howard Eastman competed from 1994 to 2014 and fought at the middleweight world championships level. He also held the British, Commonwealth and EBU European middleweight titles twice, each between 1998 and 2007.

The Guyanese-British pugilist had spent some time amongst the ranks of the homeless and later served in the Gulf War with the Royal Fusiliers. Howard was an almighty character who promoter Frank Warren described as "boxing's best-kept secret." He sported a white goatee beard and was rarely seen without his

131

ferocious pet parrot Tyson! His girlfriend (Howard's, not the parrot) also became a client of Jonathan Power Associates – the best-selling author Shaa Wasmund. While still at university, she had promoted Chris Eubank's fight with Nigel Benn, the biggest fight to ever take place in Britain at the time. They made up quite an ensemble!

I used to enjoy visiting the gym down the Old Kent Road where Howard would go through his gruelling work-out. I would sit quietly and watch, accompanied by the parrot. Howard often put me to work as an unofficial timekeeper, counting down the minutes and ringing the bell at the end of each 'round.' Joe Calzaghe also made similar use of me. Perhaps I had found my true vocation?

The wily Howard knew how to earn a crust. Boxing was "all about money," he told the *Independent* newspaper. Put on a good show and you will earn plenty of money, was his advice. He was another example of someone who was prepared to work hard to make a go of things.

Howard never quite achieved the status to which he aspired, though not for want of trying - entering the ring to face undisputed Middleweight Champion Bernard Hopkins in February 2005 in Los Angeles. I attended this bout as Howard's guest alongside his banker Andy Stubbs. Despite taking the champion the distance, the Battersea Bomber was convincingly defeated on points by Hopkins, who was making his 20th defence of the title.

That trip to LA was a great experience, as we rubbed shoulders with legends of the ring such as Thomas "the Hitman" Hearns, Zab Judah and Floyd Mayweather Senior. I also recall encountering an up-and-coming Carl Froch, who later held multiple world titles in the super-middleweight division.

It was a particular thrill to meet and chat with Emanuel Steward out there. The late Emanuel" Manny" Steward was known as the Godfather of Detroit Boxing, having trained 41 world champion fighters throughout his career.

Most notably Hearns, the famous Kronk Gym, and later

heavyweights Lennox Lewis and Wladimir Klitschko.

These were some of the spin-offs from the hard work we put in to ensure that our clients received the absolute best service from us. They certainly seemed to appreciate the fact that we would often go above and beyond what would normally be expected, and the rewards could be spectacular.

The sports stars came from across a broad spectrum. From football, rugby, boxing, snooker, cricket, golf and athletics. Sometimes the comings and goings at our offices resembled scenes from *World of Sport* or *Grandstand*!

In 2003, I formed another company to sit alongside Jonathan Power Associates. The new outfit would offer clients property investment opportunities with well-known developers based in central London. Jonathan Power Properties Ltd. was a separate entity from Jonathan Power Associates.

The new enterprise became a great success. JPP promoted a handful of developments in the heart of the capital. Our first location was on the Albert Embankment, opposite the Houses of Parliament. The development offered a mix of 1 and 2-bedroom apartments in the former home of Decca Records. The same Decca Records that once rejected The Beatles. The area was ripe for development. The US Embassy relocated to a nearby site as part of an extensive regeneration programme. Many sporting stars invested in this prestigious development, and we collaborated closely with them to deliver their investment strategy. We sought to obtain the best off-plan deals for our clients, consulting with agents, lawyers, accountants, and other members of their supporting teams.

Team meetings were also crucial. These took place with my own staff but also with clients and their representatives. I relished working in this way, collaborating with partners to ensure that we were all singing from the same hymn sheet. I relished working in this way, collaborating, communicating, and encouraging others.

As the area around Battersea Power Station became the subject of more development, we secured some very favourable arrangements with the developer, exclusively for our clients at the fashionable Chelsea Bridge Wharf development. A full furniture pack, 2-year rental payment schemes and other benefits were on offer. As I now contemplate the current value of these properties, I can't help but reflect on the price for which we secured them. It seems a real bargain now, such has been the rise in property prices in that part of London. I have first-hand knowledge of this as I even secured a few properties for myself, which I still retain.

During these times, I also marketed a property development in Chelsea called Grosvenor Waterside. It sat on the River Thames located at Chelsea Bridge, next to Chelsea Barracks and a short walk from Sloane Square. I became involved with the developer at the early stage of the build process. My company JPP Ltd was given the opportunity to market the development. It was a development with a huge potential for medium to long-term capital growth.

Since marketing the project, the gains for clients who had retained their properties have been significant. Not only that, but there were greater benefits again to be had, as the neighbouring development at Chelsea Barracks has become one of the most highly-priced addresses in central London. As they say, when buying a property there are three simple rules that a buyer should consider. Location, location, location.

JPP was not committed or tied down to providing or promoting a certain type of property. We obtained our commission on each sale that arose from our introduction. The business was booming as clients old and new clamoured for these glitzy apartments in sought-after parts of one of the world's most exciting cities. They were heady times for us to be sure. It all seemed such a far cry from my days peddling telegrams around the Cardiff streets.

After a few years of trading, we instigated an internal restructuring of the company on the advice of our corporate adviser. This arose from the view that the organisation needed a more corporate look and feel, rather than being seen as my own personal vehicle. A change of name would also help reinforce the new company image.

The company was rebranded as Property & Investment Power with a new limited liability partnership also being formed.

The nature of the business remained largely unchanged. We kept advice in-house, with a small number of support staff and two Independent Financial Advisers. The business retained its place as a market leader with an impressive client base and a healthy balance sheet. We were on a very sound commercial and financial footing indeed, having surpassed all our initial expectations. Turnover and profits were healthy, to say the least.

Annual reviews with our accountants and bankers ensured that this momentum was sustained, and our business processes remained sound. The sums we paid out in corporation tax alone were testament to our financial standing.

As you can see, the clients we worked alongside came from the very top of the sporting tree.

World champions, Olympic legends, household names from household games. Decorated sporting icons. Sporting nobility.

Glittering names from all kinds of games. It was like the old 70s TV show *Superstars* at times, as we made important connections with elite athletes from right across the sporting arena.

Setting aside the stardust and the glamour though, had I been right to turn down that opportunity from Kingsbridge? Had I backed my own instinct and judgement wisely?

It had been a very tempting offer but the decision to plough my own furrow had proved to be the right one. I had superseded the Kingsbridge offer by a considerable margin. My reputation was firmly established across the whole sector. I had brought considerable opportunities for the multitude of sporting and entertainment stars we helped before I retired.

The money was in the banks of a great many people thanks to our efforts.

As someone once said…*"show me the money!"*

My World of Entertainment

"There's no business like show business.
No business I know.
Everything about it is appealing…"

If I had occasionally pinched myself as I contemplated the Premier League superstars, world boxing champions, rugby legends, Olympians, and wizards of the snooker cue that I had represented, then my encounters with the bright lights of stage & screen took me to another level. The roar of the crowd; the smell of the grease paint.

As my career branched out from sports stars, I encountered the very biggest names from the world of show business. From 1999 until retirement, I enjoyed repeat business with A-list clients. Sometimes I really had to steel myself as global celebrities sought my advice.

In this chapter, I look back at some of my top showbiz clients. Names to set the jaw-dropping. From Haverfordwest to Hollywood.

I provided financial advice to some of the highest-profile stars around. Their services were in high demand. As my role later further grew into theatre production, my own star simply rose and rose in the firmament.

Hurray for Hollywood.

Before I begin though, some context is required. These guys are at the top of the tree. The very top.

They are top though for a reason. That reason is hard work. Hard work by the stars themselves but also, hard work by their agents, advisors and representatives.

Hard work on the part of people like Jonathan Power Associates Ltd.

It is called show 'business' for a reason.

When you see an artist perform, there is so much work that takes place behind the scenes before the lights go on. Before the curtain goes up.

Lionel Richie doesn't just rock up at the Encore Theatre Las Vegas, grab the mike, and belt out the hits. It may look 'easy like a Sunday morning' but believe me, a lot of guys press a lot of buttons to deliver these super shows.

Whether recording a song, performing on stage, or shooting a film on location, it's all the same. In the words of one of my favourite guys, the late, great, Lemmy from Motörhead, "playing for the high one; the Ace of Spades". The former Hawkwind star even bought me a whisky on my stag night in Stringfellows in London!

Hard, hard work.

…and the colour of show business is green. Yankee dollar green.

I worked with a wealth of clients and their representatives. Without breaking client confidentiality, the advice from myself and my team spanned the spectrum of financial decision-making: mortgages, ISAs, taxation, and pensions. The repeat business we generated helped secure the financial wherewithal of some of the very biggest names out there. The names in this chapter all benefited from the advice my team provided.

My musical contacts came from a single source. Prager Metis is a top 50 U.S. accounting firm and a top 10 international firm. They work diligently to uphold their reputation as their clients' trusted go-to advisor, bringing a unique level of expertise and global presence to serve a diverse domestic and international clientele.

Prager and Fenton began in New York City in 1920. The firm focused on the entertainment and music industry boasting Irving Berlin, Mary Pickford, and even Charlie Chaplin amongst their earliest clients. As the music industry switched its emphasis to London and Hollywood, they adapted, opening offices in both locations. This allowed the firm to continue to serve its growing international client base.

In 2013, the firm combined Metis Group LLC to form Prager Metis. The two outfits found their deep-rooted practices to be

137

complementary. The Metis Group provided a full range of accounting and tax services, setting a trajectory of tremendous growth that, even today, has shown no signs of slowing down.

To quote their famous line, Prager Metis, "Your World. Worth More".

These were my kind of guys.

As I contemplated some of the names I worked with, a wry smile came across my lips.

Imagine an awards ceremony for these characters, I mused. The whole red-carpet treatment where I hand out prestigious awards which recognise the absolute best in each category of the entertainment business that I encountered.

This chapter could be fun.

Oh, and yes, Emma and Millie, you get to wear new frocks.

Best Musical Performance

I have been fortunate enough to work with and around some of the top names from the pop charts across a range of genres.

Kim Appleby enjoyed a string of hits in the 80s as part of a double act with her sister Mel. A most 'respectable' chart track record you might say. When Mel sadly passed away in 1993 after losing her battle with cancer aged only 23, Kim continued as a solo artist with top 10 hits in the 90s.

I also enjoyed a close professional association with Caron Wheeler, a pioneer of the British soul scene from the iconic band Soul II Soul. Soul II Soul set the pace for laid-back, husky vocals with hits and awards in the UK and USA.

I recall enjoying one of my clients Dee Lewis performing her hit song "The Best of my Love" on TV. She later teamed up with Jamiroquai. I was used to seeing my clients on *Match of the Day* or *Football Focus* but now here they were on *Top of the Pops!*

My award though goes to a giant of the prog rock era.

With record sales in the millions, Emerson Lake and Palmer achieved enormous success in a crowded market - as psychedelia evolved into elaborate and complex 'progressive' musical creations.

Their line-up included the influential Greg Lake, with whom I worked closely later in his life.

Lake has an impressive pedigree in the rock world, having served an apprenticeship with the legendary King Crimson. Their 1969 album *In the Court of the Crimson King* was inspired by free-form jazz and other genres. The vocals and bass-playing of Greg Lake rescued the album from occasional moments of self-indulgence as prog rock began to form itself. Check out the amazing album cover too. *Brain Salad Surgery* would not be far behind!

As ELP threatened world domination, their combination of classical music, infused with jazz and rock was an almighty platform for the late musical maestro. Greg Lake produced all the band's work, including a 1971 re-working of Mussorgsky's "Pictures at an Exhibition" composition, which was recorded live. The eclectic mix of complex musical arrangements and frenetic keyboards summed up the music of the time. Lake later teamed up with other giants of the music business – The Who, Ringo Starr, Asia, and Cozy Powell. Such was the status of being the L in ELP.

Moreover, just imagine Christmas without his 1975 hit, "I Believe in Father Christmas?" That track alone – which bemoans the commercialisation of Christmas – has been covered by Robbie Williams, Elaine Page, Toyah Willcox, and Susan Boyle amongst others.

In 2016, Rolling Stone magazine described how ELP evolved to become a "stadium-filling phenomenon" thanks to a string of huge albums. Their innovative reworking of Aaron Copeland's "Fanfare for the Common Man" became the third best-selling instrumental track ever, though the 10-minute album version was shaved for the singles market.

In the monsters of rock world of the '70s and beyond, Greg Lake was a towering beast.

Best Performance in a Radio Show

I am going to go a little off-piste here.

Outside of Wales, there is a chance that you may never have heard of this chap.

Within Welsh borders though, he is a household name. If you are "in the Garden" you know all about Chris Needs.

Chris was born in Cwmafan near Port Talbot in 1954.

Before joining Radio Wales, he was a presenter for independent Welsh radio. He built up a large and loyal following with his cheerful one-to-one style. In 1996's Radio 'Oscars' he won the coveted Sony Silver Award for Best Regional Presenter.

For 18 years Chris delivered his own brand of late-night music and chat with the Friendly Garden Programme, where he formed an on-air club of listeners. Listeners could join the garden, and each had a membership number.

In 2005, Chris Needs was awarded the MBE. Some of the garden club members were even there with him to celebrate his momentous day.

Fellow Welsh broadcaster Mal Pope described a gig at the Grand Pavilion Porthcawl. Chris passed away in 2020. Mal had earlier been invited by Chris Needs. This was one of his famous 'Garden Parties.' The room was full of his BBC Radio Wales 'Garden Members' and the stage was full of artists that Chris championed on his Radio Show. A wonderful tribute.

Chris was unique, offering companionship and comfort to a late-night audience. In between tracks from a diverse and eclectic mix ranging from, I don't know, AC/DC to Shirley Bassey, or euro disco from Chris' beloved Benidorm, you might find Chris taking a call in the late hours, from a lonely, perhaps vulnerable listener. They were compelling exchanges between friends who might never meet.

Chris' listeners regarded him as a genuine friend, a role he played with grace and humility. The show featured his husband Gabe (who I also advised) and even his dog Buster (who I didn't). As a demonstration of public service broadcasting, 'Chris Needs'

Friendly Garden' was top drawer. It's not always about platinum discs or multi million pound film deals. "Gwneud y pethau bach," said St David.

Do the Little Things.

TV Times Award!

Although I am long since retired from the financial world, it remains a source of pride that many of the people I worked with have gone from strength to strength. Many of the names I assisted continue to crop up on the big screen or the small one.

Phil Collinson has a historic list of credits to his name.

Originally an actor, he later became a script editor and writer. His CV reads like a route map around the staple TV diet of the nation. After writing for *Emmerdale,* he moved on to produce *Peak Practice, Doctor Who* and *Coronation Street.* Phil has shaped the nation's viewing habits like no other man.

Collinson has spoken frankly about the appeal of Dr. Who to the gay community. The asexual Time Lord was a fantasy character, who appealed easily to gay men, he felt. As an actor, Collinson played Alexander in the 1999 TV drama *Queer as Folk,* written by his close friend Russell T Davies.

In the new millennium, Phil produced the enormously popular, yet challenging, TV drama, *It's a Sin.* The show dealt with the growth of HIV and AIDS in the 80s. Welsh writer Russell T Davies offered some jaw-dropping viewing in the series. A teen audience who later grappled with Coronavirus may have had a limited understanding of the origins of this killer disease and its impact on an unprepared gay community. Collinson and Davies put a stop to that in a matter of episodes.

The drama centred around five friends whose lives were tested by the shadow of AIDS, yet they lived and loved with eye-watering ferocity.

At times, the scenes were graphic, at times poignant. A superb cast delivered an emotional portrayal of sometimes

141

difficult and uncomfortable viewing. Millions and millions tuned in as TV-watching entered a new world of binge viewing. Viewers watched in their own time and space, as lockdown provided the ideal excuse for marathon sessions in front of the flat-screen TV. Even *Coronation Street, EastEnders,* and *Emmerdale,* for so long the soaps which anchored the weekly viewing schedules, have started dropping a week's worth of episodes online.

It's a Sin was a world away from the cosy, fireside viewing of *Emmerdale* though, with its soundtrack featuring Blondie, Culture Club, and, of course, the Pet Shop Boys. The show picked up the prize of Best Series at the Monte Carlo Television Festival in 2021. Lydia West also collected an award for best actress for her role as Jill Baxter.

TV would rarely be the same again.

Best Crossover Artist

Elsewhere in this book, I refer to the footballing credentials of John Fashanu. Fash, you recall, made a name for himself as the 'take-no-prisoners' hard-man of the famous Wimbledon FC Crazy Gang.

When Fash hung up his boots though, he reinvented himself as a TV personality.

He became a feature of Saturday night TV in the 90s, presenting the highly popular sports entertainment game show *Gladiators* alongside the lovely Ulrika Jonsson. At its prime, *Gladiators* could attract around 14 million viewers.

He entered the jungle during the second series of *I'm a Celebrity ...Get Me Out of Here*, finishing runner-up in 2003. Other TV shows followed.

John's career later took him to Nigeria, as a presenter of *Deal or No Deal.* He began presenting the Nigerian version of the show at the same time as Noel Edmonds did in the UK. It became massively popular in a country with a population of 211 million people and Fash worked hard to make sure he improved in the role, watching himself on the show to improve his technique. (There's that 'hard work' ethic again, see?)

If you are unsure about how this show worked, the basic format is that contestants would open a series of boxes to discover which box held the big money prize. Fash describes his joy at seeing how people who were not affluent suddenly came into money on the show. He was helping them to a new start in life.

Fash the Bash had become Fash the Cash!

Lifetime Achievement Award

On leaving the world of financial advice, I later branched out into the world of showbiz as a theatrical producer, joining forces for example with the Lythgoe family to take pantomime to the United States of America, staging productions in Los Angeles. This was an innovative venture for sure. Pantomime and the Midwest USA aren't natural bedfellows, I promise you.

My interaction with major TV, sports, and entertainment made this a natural progression. I moved from a 'behind-the-scenes' confidant to a front-of-house figure.

The achievement of this stardust-littered lifetime though, was working with the magnificent Idina Menzel.

Quite simply, Idina Menzel is a Broadway great. Her instantly recognisable vocal style has elevated her to the very top of the tree. It would be hard to overstate her sheer magnitude. Stars really don't shine brighter than this.

Idina's CV reads like the diary of a teen idol. She has starred in *Glee, Wicked* and *Enchanted*. She has sold out Madison Square Garden and sang "The Star-Spangled Banner" at The Super Bowl. Album sales, TV shows, Tony Awards. When young girls fall asleep at night dreaming of a career in show business, Idina Menzel is who they want to be.

I was thrilled to jointly produce her show at the Royal Albert Hall. It sold out. A UK tour followed. To produce such a major international star was the pinnacle of the later stages of my career.

As any self-respecting 10-year-old knows though, Idina is really Elsa, the beautiful star of the smash Disney animation film, *Frozen*. Immortalised and captured forever in a Disney world of ice. Walt would have been so proud.

That single film immortalised Menzel. It became the highest-grossing animated film of all time, and one of the highest-grossing films of all time. Her performance of the iconic "Let it Go" track, won an Academy Award and a Grammy Award. It was nominated for a Golden Globe Award. The role of Elsa has seen her advance into video games and further films which, inevitably, include *Frozen II*.

Like so many of the stars I encountered though, there was also another side to Idina Menzel. She is a long-standing champion of LGBT rights and has also collaborated with Justin Bieber and others to celebrate Earth Day. A role model for many, Idina has been honoured with a star on the Hollywood Walk of Fame. Her star sits alongside Julie Andrews, Frank Sinatra, Michael Jackson, Marilyn Monroe, and even Mickey Mouse.

Idina is a worthy winner of the imaginary 'lifetime achievement' award, though I think my success in promoting such a huge international star at a venue like the Royal Albert Hall was quite an achievement of its own!

Best Songwriter

Now, this was a toughie. No wonder I left it until last. Some of these were amongst my most wealthy clients,

As they say at the BAFTAs and Oscars, "Here is the list of nominees… "

Al Clay

I was always going to like Al, wasn't I?

Like me, he began his professional life as a tea boy – at London's Trident Studios – to progress through the music business via engineering, mixing, and production. He has worked with Pink, The Stereophonics, and Del Amitri. In a career that has spanned rock through pop and film, his CV includes *The Da Vinci Code, Pirates of the Caribbean, Batman Begins,* and even *The Simpsons!*

Al's company, Westside Pacific Music, is a state-of-the-art recording studio and artist development company in Southern California. Their artist development program nurtures new talent into a professional and cohesive product, with links to record labels, publishers, etc.

Richard "Biff" Stannard

Richard "Biff" Stannard, founded the songwriting team 'Biffco' with my other clients Julian Gallagher and Ash Howes, in Brighton. The productive outfit has worked with the highest of high-profile chart acts.

Just look at these names for a flavour of the artists who have used their services:

One Direction
Will Young
The Saturdays
Westlife
U2
Kylie Minogue
Little Mix

Stannard helped bring the Spice Girls to the nation's hearts in the 90s as the girls went on to sell more than 75 million records. Their first hit, "Wannabe" – written by Stannard in collaboration with the band members and another client Matt Rowe – topped the charts in an amazing 37 countries.

Stannard has also enjoyed success as a show song producer on *The X Factor.* 20 million viewers tuned in as *The X Factor* set the pace for TV viewing, talent spotting, and producing hit records.

When chart history is written again, Stannard will be at the top. At one stage in his remarkable career, the UK top 10 included six songs produced by the amazing Richard Stannard.

Martin Harrington

Martin Harrington's client list includes some of the very biggest names in pop. He has written songs for Celine Dion, Stevie Wonder, Ed Sheeran, Emma Bunton, Five, Natalie Imbruglia, and Blue.

As of 2021, Céline Dion's net worth was approximately $800 million. One of the richest singers in the world. Ed Sheeran? Well, you can Google him yourself maybe. This was pop music on another level. In the words of Blue, "all rise" for Mr Martin Harrington.

Harrington's story, incidentally, also includes a $20m run-in with Ed Sheeran over his single "Photograph." Harrington and American Thomas Leonard claim it has a similar structure to their own song, "Amazing." The duo claimed that Sheeran's ballad had the same musical composition as their track, which was released by former X Factor winner Matt Cardle in 2012. Sheeran settled out of court.

***

I guess the relevance of all these anecdotes to my own tale is that they simply underline the magnitude of the clients I advised and supported.

The timeline from Greg Lake to *The X-Factor* virtually spans the entire history of rock and roll. Idina Menzel is an idol to a pre-teen Disney generation. John Fashanu straddles the whole spectrum of my professional career like a colossus, elbowing his way to the top, making the most of his opportunities and talents.

Ok, you may not boast the songwriting talent of Biff Stannard, the technical ability of Greg Lake or the creativity of Phil Collinson .... but perhaps you have the will to win of John

Fashanu, the warmth of Chris Needs, or the sheer vibrancy of Kim Appleby or Caron Wheeler. The toolbox of success is deep and wide. Just make the most of yourself. That's all I ask.

In 2011, Biff Stannard told Pink News "We were working 18-hour days, seven days a week. We wrote Wannabe quite quickly, but it took ages to get it to sound right. I remember waking up on the studio floor with this post-it from Matt saying, 'Press play.' We'd finally got it. So, it was luck and hard work."

Through hard work, you can sometimes make your own luck. Believe me.

Oh, and the winner of my imaginary songwriter award? Well, it must be Al Clay, mustn't it.

After all, us tea boys must stick together.

Exit Strategy

Away from the workplace, life was good.

A contented and relaxed husband, I had embarked on married life with my fiancé Emma Bonas. Our precious and beloved daughter Millie arrived in 2004.

My client base resembled a 'who's who' of the sporting and entertainment elite.

I was so proud to count Sir Bobby Robson and Sir Geoff Hurst as ambassadors of my commercial undertakings, a role they performed with dignity and commitment. My social calendar even included royal engagements, such as Viscount Linley who invited me to his Christmas parties.

David Albert Charles Armstrong-Jones, 2nd Earl of Snowdon styled as Viscount Linley until 2017, and known professionally as David Linley, made progress in the commercial world as a furniture maker. He is a former chairman of the auction house Christie's UK. As the son of Princess Margaret and Antony Armstrong-Jones, 1st Earl of Snowdon, he was fifth in the line of succession to the throne at his birth.

Fifth.

As of September 2022, he is 24th in line to the throne and the first person who is not a direct descendant of the Monarch. He was nephew to HM Queen Elizabeth II. Auntie Lillibett, I expect.

My association with David stemmed from meeting him at a business function. We soon established a commercial relationship and enjoyed meeting up at his Belgravia HQ. David had established his own furniture business with an elite client base. He was keen to explore potential opportunities for referrals from my glittering client base.

Yes, you read that correctly.

Royalty was now asking the kid from Haverfordwest to send some business their way if that was ok with the kid. The Establishment came to me to ask about the prospect of referrals and collaborations.

The lad who had been rejected and doubted by so many others was now sat at the top table. The very top.

David's parties were immense. These were no sausage-on-stick buffets with a few cans of warm lager I can tell you, as the Viscount proved an extremely agreeable host, even introducing me to his father, Lord Snowdon with humility, which did him great credit. Yes, David, I know who your father is!

Special times indeed.

In 2006, I was nominated for the much-coveted Entrepreneur of the Year Award, sponsored by the Financial Times, Coutts Bank, the London Stock Exchange and Ernst & Young.

Ernst & Young Global Limited is a London-based, multinational professional services network. One of the largest professional services networks in the world, it is considered one of the 'big four' accounting firms along with Deloitte, KPMG, and PricewaterhouseCoopers. The Ernst & Young Entrepreneur awards programme was an acknowledgement of the contribution that entrepreneurs made, not just to business but to society as a whole and the risks they took in doing so.

This filled me with pride. It wasn't an award that one could apply for and was reliant upon being recognised by others for success. To think that my achievements came to the attention of such an eminent assortment of commentators and distinguished financial practitioners was a wonderful endorsement of my personal success and that of my team. I was humbled at the recognition.

The process featured diligence tests and dialogue. I discovered that my Bank Manager at Coutts, David Palser nominated me for the prestigious accolade. He believed that I had a great chance of winning the award due to the success I had achieved in taking my business from a standing start, to the heights we reached.

During the interview that took place as part of the assessment process, I mentioned that I was looking to retire in the next few years. This was met with some surprise as I remember. I was still only 42 after all. There was astonishment that I was prepared to turn my back on everything at such a young age and after so little time in the hot seat. Should I not be looking to expand?

I was content with my achievements though. I explained that I had easily achieved my own ambitions and surpassed my expectations. From humble origins, I now wanted to go out at the top and on my own terms. Like the great Welsh rugby union legend Barry John perhaps.

It later emerged that I had earned a top four spot in the awards. Semi-finalist. My framed 2006 certificate sits proudly in my study these days. It remains one of my proudest possessions and a testimony to the drive, ambition and dedication of myself and my team.

From the feedback I received, it seems that had I not indicated a wish to retire but showed a desire to achieve new targets, then my study might be decorated with a winner's certificate rather than a semi-finalist award.

I was incredibly happy with the award though. I had been true to myself and approached the assessment with honesty and integrity. Despite the shock felt by those around me at the announcement of my intentions, I knew my own thoughts. I knew that I wanted to be my own man, even in retirement.

As I have mentioned, my business had been my hobby and my hobby had been my business.

In time though, this ceased to be the case and the lure of retirement proved to be strong.

Had I continued I may have extended my relationship with Terry Waite with whom I had discussed some opportunities to develop a charitable arm for my business.

Terry had been an assistant to Robert Runcie, Archbishop of Canterbury during the 80s. As an envoy to the Church of England, he visited Lebanon to negotiate the release of four hostages but ended up as a hostage himself. He was detained in that capacity for four years. After his release, he became known for his association with charitable causes and humanitarian work.

Over the years I had supported many charities through the donation of signed memorabilia from my sporting clients. They were more than happy to support a worthy cause by signing the odd shirt. It was an area I was extremely interested to extend, as I looked back on my successful career. Giving something back? If that's how you want to think of it, yes. Terry was interested in the concept, as you might expect.

The long spells away from Emma and Millie had meant that, in later years, it became more important for me to enjoy quality time with the family. I enjoyed the daily school run and wanted to be around while Millie grew up, not spend so much of my time pounding the motorways to head up to London, Birmingham, or Manchester. Don't get me wrong, it had been an exhilarating and rewarding career but as my young family grew, I could now afford to have other priorities. This was why I had worked so hard, after all.

To use a cricketing analogy, it was a long, slow walk back to the pavilion, but I was ready to declare my innings. The scoreboard told its own tale as I hung up the bat.

I took the eventual decision to finally retire and began to plan my exit. This would need careful handling if I was to protect my investments and set up my future.

Ernst & Young – of all people – approached me to discuss the sale of my company. I would need to work closely with their London-based mergers and acquisition team. This wouldn't happen overnight. On their advice, I also brought in an experienced consultant with the accounting skills I needed to oversee the arrangements.

For the first time since I don't know when, I was now spending considerable chunks of time away from the workplace, content to let others run the show as I devoted more time to Emma and Millie.

In hindsight, perhaps I should have paid closer attention, rather than leave the running of my business in the hands of those who did not possess the emotional attachment to the company which I had established. I took more and more of a back step, as my consultant also did the heavy lifting and implemented the

151

complex, time-consuming deal, liaising with Ernst & Young along the way.

After several months, once the due diligence tests were complete, it became apparent that, if I were to sell the business, I would remain tied into any sale agreement for at least three years. This would have meant that, effectively, I would have continued to work for any company which bought me.

I saw echoes of my Kingsbridge experiences here, when there had been interest in acquiring my assets when the company was still in its infancy. This was not the way I planned my exit at all.

I informed Ernst & Young that I was not interested in this type of arrangement. I therefore contacted my clients, thanked them for their business and loyalty and informed them, quite simply, that I would be retiring. End of.

I ensured that my staff received favourable remuneration terms and, for a short term, helped to establish Power Goldberg, a sports management team who concluded transfer arrangements for leading footballers. We did deals at clubs such as Derby County, Everton and West Bromwich Albion amongst others.

In an interesting post-script to these episodes, I recall receiving a call from Mel Goldberg, my fellow director at Power Goldberg.

Mel had received an approach from ZigZag Productions. They were interested in putting on a TV series to be called Super Agents.

The reality show would pit six budding young entrepreneurs against each other for the prize of a contract with our company. The series would air on prime-time weekend TV and feature a similar format to *The Apprentice*.

Jamie Carragher, Emmanuel Adebayor and Kanu were among the Premier League stars set to appear in the show.

Carragher would kick things off in the initial episode by explaining to the young candidates what a star player required from an agent. They would then be sent to the club's Academy to assess who they considered would be the best choice as a client.

The daughter of colourful ex-Liverpool goalkeeper Bruce Grobbelaar, Tahli, was to play a key part in the show. She was also one of our employees alongside Jamaican soccer international Fitzroy Simpson, who also featured in the show.

Each week, La Grobbelaar and Fitz would set the competitors a task, such as scouting talent at a youth football match at Liverpool's Academy. Tahli and Fitz would then report back to boss Mel Goldberg advising him of their progress up to the point of elimination. As I say, think *The Apprentice.*

Power Goldberg was thus a major stakeholder in this entire venture through the involvement of Mel, Tahli and Fitzroy Simpson. Our name was all over the show. I had spent a lifetime creating the reputation which underpinned that name. Goldberg was excited by the project and the enormous PR benefits it would bring. I could see this, but I saw a missing ingredient. There was to be no payment to us. I enjoyed my work, but I didn't work for free. I didn't believe that Power Goldberg should either.

I recall the meeting when things came to a head. It would cost ZigZag £50,000 to use our name, our director and two of our staff, I announced.

Tense glances flashed across the room. Phone calls in corridors. Whispers in the shadows.

The guys from ZigZag blinked first.

"It's a deal, Mr Power," they said.

The paperwork was drawn up and the cash made its way to the Power Goldberg coffers. Not a penny came to me. It was my parting gift to the company.

I announced my retirement from the sporting world shortly afterwards.

Don't sell yourself short guys, there are plenty out there waiting to take advantage.

This was all a nice swansong but my days as the real-life Jerry Maguire had ended. The high-powered world would have to manage without me. My days as a confidant and adviser to the stars of sport and entertainment were at an end. The Fat Lady cleared her throat. JP exited stage-left.

Extra! Extra! Read All About It!

I had contacted most former clients to advise them of my retirement from the financial world that had occupied so much of my attention for so long. It still took several months for my phone to stop ringing though, as the long path of retirement stretched ahead of me.

My business persona diminished as my corporate advisers closed my financial corporate structure, and served notice of my retirement to the Financial Services Authority.

For the first time in some 20 years, I was free to explore pastures new. I could think of myself now.

My initial priorities included spending quality time with my family. The little things in life gave me new pleasure. The school run with Millie for example, as I threw myself into normal family life. We holidayed abroad regularly as a family, even taking in a test match between the West Indies and England on a Caribbean trip. Old habits die hard, I guess!

I was able to sit back now and contemplate my own future, having spent many years safeguarding the future of others. It was time for some much-needed head candy.

I owned a portfolio of London apartments purchased during my time in the financial sector. I decided that I would self-manage each property that my staff had previously run on my behalf. I retain this role today and it's one I enjoy. The old grey matter needs some stimulation of course and I still derive much pleasure from providing these quality opportunities for London living. I guess it satisfies that business drive that still lingers within me.

The space in my head that now existed also allowed me to satisfy my love of the arts.

Performance and drama had always appealed to me from a young age. Really though, I longed to poke behind the scenes a little to try to obtain a feel for how it all operated. Who ran the show? Who called the shots? Who pulled the strings – and I don't mean the strings that brought the final curtain down at the end of the night after the fat lady had done her bit?

We enjoyed many trips as a family to the West End and the New Theatre in our hometown of Cardiff.

I loved the world of theatre. I was fascinated by how it all worked. The atmosphere within a crowded auditorium also held a special appeal for me. It pulled me in and held my attention. I would marvel at the skills of the actors on stage and their performances beneath the lights. How I wished that were me up there. "Alas poor Power, I knew him well!"

I decided that it was time to pursue a new interest. A hobby, even.

Yes, a hobby would be good. I held no interest in returning to the business world I had left behind.

Or so I thought.

My interest in performing seemed to offer the opportunity I sought. I saw myself as a film extra maybe to begin with. I could be 'bloke in the pub' or 'third soldier in the mud' I mused. I decided to approach some acting agencies to try to join their books. It was worth a punt to amuse me I thought. I had been at the very top of the tree for so long that starting back at the beginning of the ladder held some appeal somehow. The quiet anonymity would also be welcome after a life in the fast lane.

I knew that there would be opportunities out there. The BBC had recently established a new studio in the revamped Cardiff Bay and major shows such as *Casualty* and even *Dr Who* were now delivered from the Welsh capital. I wasn't sure I saw myself as a Dalek or Cyberman, but it was certainly a world for which I was ready.

Philip Collinson, the television producer I had dealt with in the past, agreed that some work as a TV or film 'Extra' would be an enjoyable introduction to the world of performing arts.

Little did we both know where this would lead.

After being taken on by a few film and TV extra agencies, my 'acting' debut was set for the TV series *Sherlock*, starring Benedict Cumberbatch.

In accordance with strict instructions, I turned up at the location on time. Filming would take place at the Bush Inn, a delightful Grade II listed public house in St Hilary, near Cowbridge, in the leafy surroundings of the Vale of Glamorgan just to the west of Cardiff.

The current inn dates to the 16th century. It features a thatched roof, thick stone walls, low oak beams, pews, stone floors, a stone spiral staircase, and an inglenook fireplace. This was the life, I thought. Life as an Extra would be just up my street. I quickly learned some harsh lessons mind.

My fellow performers made it noticeably clear to me that we were not 'Extras.' The correct term was 'Supporting Artists.' They were proud of their contribution to these immensely popular TV shows. I found that out straight away.

I also soon came to appreciate that there was a definite hierarchy to the world of Ext…Supporting Artists.

Many of my new colleagues had undertaken the role for some 20 years. They were only too pleased to share their stories with all and sundry. Some of these guys took name-dropping to new levels as I shared the set with 'stars' of many top shows. That bloke playing darts in Queen Vic, the guy waiting patiently to be served in the Rovers Return. The dolly bird sat behind Del in the Nag's Head? This was TV royalty, of sorts.

This was all good stuff of course and I am sure the names and the stories would have impressed many. For my part though, I was much more interested in the behind-the-scenes action. I was fascinated by how it all worked. Amazed at the number of staff involved. Eager young things fresh from college, experienced film crews, sound engineers, make-up artists, production staff, guys with scripts, actors I knew from the TV, and some who, well it was difficult to see just what they did, to be honest. Everybody was remarkably busy though. A place for everyone and everyone in their place.

"Action!"

I walked into the pub on cue. Cool as cue, even. Just as I would one day walk down the red carpet I thought. "The award

156

for Best Supporting Artist in a TV drama goes to......"

To the slight annoyance of some of my fellow artists, my walk-on role required me to walk next to Sherlock Holmes himself. I would be "in the shot" as we actors (!) say. On the television for real even. Millie would be impressed!

Maybe this was just beginner's luck but, as ever, I was never one to decline what fate might put in front of me. Or at least, give it some consideration. Walking into a pub was something I had done hundreds of times. Frankly, it wasn't a role that stretched me. Nevertheless, I thoroughly enjoyed the whole experience.

When the daily filming ritual ended, each of us was required to complete the appropriate documentation to secure our fee. No form, no fee. The daily rate was £85. That felt like decent remuneration for just walking into a bar. Lunch was also included and, if you timed it right – that is – after the actors and crew had eaten, there was usually a tidy amount left for the Supporting Artists. It might make you smirk now but a daily fee of £85 plus a free lunch is not a bad return. Arguably it equates to an annual salary approaching £25k. Not to be sniffed at. I could therefore see why some of my fellow performers had stuck with this for 20 years.

Although it was exciting to be rubbing shoulders from a distance with celebrities again, I was made firmly aware of the protocols and standards which governed the life of a Supporting Artist.

At no time, for example, were we allowed to fraternise with the main cast members or other leading figures such as the director. Photographs and autographs were also taboo. You were there to work – and so were they. This came as no surprise to me.

The car park afterwards was an interesting experience, mind. Much excited chatter and admiring glances from the supporting cast towards the top-of-the-range vehicles driven by the big stars.

"Wow, look at that swanky Aston Martin. It must belong to Benedict..."

The look on their faces when 'Man-who-walks-into-pub'

quietly took the keys from his pocket and sat behind the wheel before driving off, was priceless. It still makes me chuckle today.

I enjoyed my new hobby. The money wasn't that important to me at that stage in my life but the chance to peep behind the scenes into the acting profession fascinated me. I was very keen to learn more about how it all worked and how the shows were produced.

A former financial colleague and friend of mine, Gary McMoran, introduced me to a friend of his and of Phil Collinson – Jason Haigh-Ellery.

At our first meeting, I mentioned my interest in the Arts to Jason, referencing my curiosity for exploring behind the scenes a little. My time as a Supporting Artist had been fun and had whetted my appetite. Added to my business background though, I could foresee a bigger niche for me here. It was at least worth a conversation, I thought.

Jason was a successful, respected producer. Noting my interest, he suggested the prospect of my potential involvement in future shows, if that was a direction I could see myself pursuing.

This excited me.

Jason had a track record of putting on West End shows and enjoyed success in the worlds of film, television, and radio. His theatre credits include *Footloose the Musical, Never Forget, Yes Prime Minister, The Lady-killers, Curtains,* and *New Boy.* He had collaborated with actors such as David Tennant, Paul McGann, Sir Derek Jacobi, Peter Davison, Colin Baker, Sylvester McCoy, Simon Pegg, Sheridan Smith, David Walliams, and Matt Lucas.

Jason Haigh-Ellery was also the Managing Director of Big Finish Productions and co-producer of their *Dr Who* audio stories. He also directed and performed post-production on several Dr Who audio dramas.

He is most definitely Premier League, so to speak.

Jason was true to his word and, amazingly, offered me a role as Associate Producer on a show that he was putting on at the Royal Albert Hall, London.

This would be quite a debut for me. The star of the show was Broadway sensation Idina Menzel, Tony Award-winning star of *Wicked* and *Glee.*

New Yorker Menzel achieved fame as an actress, singer & songwriter. She is best known as Maureen in *Rent,* Elphaba in *Wicked* and as the voice of Elsa in *Frozen.* The Denver Post had called her "the Streisand of her generation," while *The New York Times* praised her as "an entertainer with a phenomenal voice. Diana Ross with ten times the stamina and lung power."

The Royal Albert Hall show was a huge success. A sell-out. Emma and Millie attended and shared a box with me. I was so proud. We took the show on the road in 2012, with extensive orchestral backing for Menzel from the USA. "Neil Eckersley for Speckulation Entertainment in association with Jason Haigh-Ellery and Jonathan Power presents."

I was back.

Sharing the limelight with household names and international stars. I was now part of the showbiz world as a theatrical producer. In return for some financial investment, an Associate Producer would be privy to the nuts and bolts of the business aspects of the production, including how the show was going, ticket sales, media interest, contractual negotiations, etc.

My business background helped me understand all this but believe me, it was no easy ride. High yield and glamour yes, but extremely high risk. Not all shows make a profit.

Investors should only put in what they can afford to lose. We were backing fast horses but in an extraordinarily strong field, with many fences of unknown height.

I had been used to rubbing shoulders with well-known names of course, but this was another level again. Party invitations came thick and fast.

Emma and I attended one memorable bash hosted by Elton John at Battersea Power Station. Stars of stage and screen all around.

Elton needs no introduction of course. Having traversed from modest sing-songwriter through the heights of glam rock to conquer America, the album charts, and Disney soundtracks, he is now simply part of rock & pop royalty.

He has been awarded five Brit Awards, including the Best British Male and Outstanding Contribution to Music. In 2013 he received the first Brits Icon award in recognition of his "lasting impact" on UK culture, which was presented to him by his close friend Rod Stewart.

Amazingly, I saw echoes of myself in Elton. Humble origins, hard work, knocks, rejection, bright lights.

Now, here I was, rubbing shoulders with Captain Fantastic.

In all, I went to three of his parties. A duet he performed with Motown legend Smokey Robinson remains a particularly memorable highlight. The private events were 'invitation only' and laid the groundwork for the Elton John AIDS Foundation. He has been knighted for his charitable work.

Elton enjoyed a business relationship with a good friend of mine Eugenia Van Der Geest. Eugenia was a confidant to many major celebrities and would throw intimate parties all over the world where guests like Elton would perform. Indeed, we first met at one of Elton's parties. She remains a friend to this day. This attractive entrepreneur simply oozes style and star quality.

It was all quite mind-blowing, and I did well to keep my feet on the ground at times. You must be seen to be at home in these surroundings though, or your credibility simply goes out of the window. Grace Jones, Plan B, Emeli Sande…just some of the names I recall meeting in those days. The late Shane Warne too, who was dating Liz Hurley at the time.

On one occasion though, I must admit that I did drop my guard.

A friend of Eugenia's joined us at our table. He turned out to be a charming and engaging guy. For once, I took my eye off the ball and confessed that my wife, who had been unable to join us that evening, truly was a big fan of his. Ordinarily, such star-struck antics would have been a definite no-no.

It was a 'careless whisper' on my part, but Mr George Michael could not have been more gracious as he autographed the

160

invitation card for the absent Mrs Power. It still enjoys pride of place at our home.

By now, a warm welcome was extended to me by the show business community. I was introduced simply as a "Producer." At one memorable function – as I awaited my complimentary drinks from a bar made entirely of ice – who should I find stood to my right - but the irrepressible Dame Shirley Bassey.

Dame Shirley is very much revered in her native Cardiff. Like many I had met on my journey, she had risen to the bright lights from humble origins. "The Girl from Tiger Bay" as she later sang.

Dame Shirley had received little support from those at her junior school at Moorland Road in Splott, Cardiff, before conquering the entertainment world thanks to her determination and talent. No wonder she struck a chord with me and after all, it isn't every day that you get to queue up at a bar with a Dame, is it?

After the very briefest of introductions on my part, Dame Shirley graciously invited me to "send regards to Cardiff" before elegantly turning away from me to resume her evening. I felt I had been granted the briefest audience with royalty. Showbiz royalty for sure. It was such a thrill.

Countless similar encounters filled my diary – I even bumped into my old friend Benedict Cumberbatch on one occasion. I decided it best not to remind him of our earlier association though!

I remained friends with another guest at our table, who had been introduced to me by Jason Haigh-Ellery at one of Elton John's parties. It was another celebrity-laden function, after which we moved on to Soho House. Roxanne Pallett had played Jo Stiles in the hit TV show *Emmerdale*. She had been nominated for several awards, including Sexiest Female, Best Storyline, and Best Actress. We enjoyed a wonderful social evening, and I referenced my earlier career to her. Contact details were exchanged and we both moved off into the London early-hours traffic.

Within a couple of weeks, Roxanne was in touch with me again. The acting superstar was keen to appraise me of a conversation she had had with the producer of her latest movie, *Devil's Tower* where she starred alongside Jason Mewes. The 2014 horror film saw Jason as a couple forced to do battle with zombies.

Roxanne had thought of my name when her producer indicated that he was looking for some film investment advice. I agreed to meet up with him and provide any advice which I thought to be appropriate.

A few weeks later, I therefore, found myself in the company of Dominic Burns, the film director, screenwriter, producer, and actor at Soho House.

Burns was a high-profile name who had worked with A-list stars such as the Muscles from Brussels Jean Claude Van Damme, the accomplished actor Richard E Grant, and Stan Lee, an American comic book writer, editor, publisher, and producer who co-created *Iron Man, The Hulk and The X-Men* who played himself in a movie directed by Burns. Burns had also directed Mark Hamill – who played Luke Skywalker in *Star Wars* – in his 2011 film *Airborne.*

There was even a nod back to my footballing days later, as Wimbledon hard man Vinnie Jones appeared in *Madness in the Method,* co-written and co-produced by Burns.

Burns was therefore a figure of some standing who I enjoyed meeting. He was young and ambitious, and I passed on what advice I could. He explained that he was about to commence directing *Allies,* an independent World War II film written by Jeremy Sheldon.

Throughout our meeting, he asked numerous questions about my life, background, and business experience but it was not until I mentioned my life-long interest in performing that the conversation really took off.

To my amazement, leading director Dominic Burns turned around and offered me a part in his film there and then.

Not just a faceless role in the background either, I would

feature alongside the stars of the film, such as Julian Ovenden, Chris Reilly, and Matt Willis. My first 'proper' acting job would see me play the part of Captain Williams. The plot told the tale of a team of British soldiers led by a US Captain, who were dropped behind enemy lines in France on a mission that could shorten the war. Commando Sergeant Harry McBain (played by Reilly) and Captain Gabriel Jackson (played by Ovenden) would be forced to set aside personal animosity if the mission was to succeed.

I accepted the role in a heartbeat.

I thoroughly enjoyed everything about the wonderful filming experience in beautiful Derbyshire, where my fellow actors made me feel completely welcome.

Sharing a dressing room with the former Busted star Matt Willis, my time on set seemed to pass in an instant, though my scenes were shot over a 12-hour period.

I had been used to the bright lights and celebrity world from my earlier career of course but these experiences were new to me.

Dominic had advised me not to let on that this was my professional acting debut. Surrounded by cast members from *Downton Abbey* and *Game of Thrones*, he felt it was important that I was treated no different from the established names rather than be brushed aside as a new boy. I had to always exude confidence to gain respect and achieve credibility.

I must have done something right I guess, as I don't recall anybody sussing out that I was a debutant. The rest of the cast and crew simply took my experience as read and I slotted right in there! It was such a thrill, believe me.

Andy Thompson, producer, writer, and filmmaker, also spoke to me one day on set and indicated that I could be just what he was looking for in relation to a forthcoming film project he was involved with.

Kicking Off was to be a football-based comedy based around two fans who try to kidnap a referee who they believe unfairly disallowed a goal which led to their team's relegation.

It sounded like a hoot. Disastrous football results were

certainly something to which I could relate having grown up supporting Cardiff City!

The characters were two lovable thugs who would leave the audience laughing and grimacing at their lack of common sense. I would feature in a scene alongside 'Wigsy' a confirmed idiot who follows the plan through with hilarious consequences.

The role of Wigsy fell to Warren Brown, one of Britain's most illustrious actors who starred alongside Idris Elba as DS Ripley, the role for which he became most well-known, in the BBC's multi-award-winning series *Luther*.

In something of a departure from my debut role as a military figure, I was asked to play the part of 'Bob the Drunk!' I could probably manage that one I thought.

During our forthcoming meetings, Andy explained how much he would like to persuade a well-known footballing icon to feature in the movie via a cameo role. Could I suggest anybody?

When I mentioned my association with Sir Geoff Hurst, Andy asked if I would agree to contact the 66 hero to see if the project might hold any appeal.

I am pleased to say that the idea very much appealed to Sir Geoff. I put the two parties in touch with one another. (Linking people to people has always been my way.)

My time on set as Bob the Drunk would take two days to film. I knew I could cut it – I had been drunk before but in fairness not for two whole days. I looked forward to the experience immensely.

Filming would take place at Selhurst Park, the home of Crystal Palace FC. I was very much at home here. Selhurst Park is a proper football ground. Palace has played there since 1924 and, on match days, there can be a special atmosphere down there in SE25.

The Holmesdale Road Stand was empty that day of course, as the makeup team set about transforming me into Bob.

What a remarkable job they performed. I was captivated by the way the guys behind the camera all played their part in putting the show together. I could see how the makeup artists, costume department, runners, and tea boys were just as vital to the overall package as leading actors and cast members – and hey, there is nothing wrong with being a tea boy is there? I knew that more than most.

Bob the Drunk was duly created. A scruffy, dishevelled vagrant, stinking of booze and slurring of speech. A down-on-his-luck victim of hard times and even harder drinking. My own mother would have failed to recognise me I reckon, such as the skill of the Greasepaint Gang.

Sir Geoff arrived on set and met up with Andy. Andy played along with a gag I had in mind to play on the former England star, as he suggested to him that a vagrant had appeared on set claiming to be a friend of Sir Geoff.

This was not what the former Hammers legend wanted to hear and began to prepare for a hasty exit. Drunken tramps tended not to knock about with world-famous footballers! I still chuckle today as I recall how we played out the charade in scenes reminiscent of *Candid Camera* or *Trigger-Happy TV*.

Anyway, we eventually lifted the covers, and Sir Geoff saw the funny side of it all when he realised the identity of the man behind the makeup. I have a great photo of us laughing together as I teased with a drunken "where did it all go wrong Geoff?" line.

This was the start of an acting career that seemed to move forward at quite a pace.

An exciting time for me saw me appear in the 2014 film *Chameleon*, a futuristic drama directed by Beau Fowler and set in a world run by a single governmental power known as the U.N.O. My role as Jack saw me perform alongside the legendary film actor Togo Igawa and Francesca Fowler from *Dr Who*.

Togo's many films and TV roles include starring alongside Tom Cruise in the 2002 American epic period action drama *The Last Samurai*. In recent years, he has appeared in major films such as *Revolver* and *Memoirs of a Geisha*. His impressive CV also includes working on *Johnny English Reborn* with Rowan Atkinson (2011), *Dr Who, Lovejoy, Casualty* and even a role as the voice of Hiro in *Thomas & Friends* (2010-16; 2020) based around the adventures of Thomas the Tank Engine! Quite a journey for someone who joined the Royal Shakespeare Company in 1968 as its first Japanese actor.

I received a degree of acclaim for my portrayal of Jack, as *Chameleon* featured at the Cannes Film Festival, the annual celebration of films of all genres held in Cannes on the Cote D'Azur. Imagine my pride at being nominated for a Jury Prize at the Focus International Film Festival. Check it out on IMDb, the online database of information for films and television series.

That was another great gig and provided a great way to help celebrate my 50th birthday on the glamorous French Riviera, alongside the Mediterranean coast of south-eastern France.

I recount all these stories now to show the importance, once again, of following your dreams and seizing the opportunity. Seize the day. You just never know where things can lead.

***

Around this time, I was approached to help with the production of a feature film called *King.*

I was immediately taken by the fabulous and moving script.

The two producers explained their ambitions for the project to me and sought my help with raising the necessary finance to deliver their plans. As I believed strongly in the project, I was happy to lend my support and assistance.

I quickly assembled a funding package to the value of £150,000. Sadly, my partners in the project failed to stump up a penny. This, I soon realised, was to be a project funded solely through my own efforts. Unfortunately, all the funds became swallowed up in "production costs" by the two producers.

Being something of a newbie in this world, I was unaware that a more effective business model would have seen the two producers invest the fund in an Escrow account – a third-party account where funds would remain until all the required funding for the film was raised. If the total funds are not raised, the money accumulated was then returned to each investor.

I still retain faith in the project though, after all this time, and would love to take the project on myself without other producers involved. I have made the other producers aware of this, though the seeds I sought to sow have fallen on stony ground.

Who knows, perhaps one day I might be granted the film rights and finally deliver *King*.

* * *

My career as a co-producer in the theatre world continued as I worked alongside Jason Haigh-Ellery.

We enjoyed a successful 25th Anniversary tour with the Scottish theatrical phenomena *The Steamie,* in partnership with Neil Laidlaw. An Anniversary Gala Night at the King's Theatre Glasgow remains a memorable highlight from May 2012. I invested a modest sum in the production, by way of seed funding.

Despite the passing of 25 years since its debut performance, Scotland's top talent still turned out in numbers for the gala performance.

Carol Smillie, Kaye Adams, Greg Hemphill, Jonathan Watson, Fred MacAulay, Paul Young, Ricky Ross, Lorraine McIntosh, Cat Harvey, and Dean Park were among those who joined show creator and writer Tony Roper at The King's Theatre, Glasgow, to celebrate the anniversary, and enjoy an evening of Scots humour and history.

The bright lights of California also came calling.

Nigel Lythgoe's family had been behind shows such as *Pop Idol* and *American Idol* and created the dance competition show, *So You Think You Can Dance.*

The family's passion lay in live performance arts. They also created non-profit projects such as the Dizzy Feet Foundation and Give Kids Panto, which focused on giving youth the opportunity to experience and create art. They are best known for creating shows for television and on stage, that the whole family could enjoy together.

I was invited to become an investor and part of the

production set-up for *Cinderella and Snow White* with Lythgoe Family Productions. I accepted the exciting challenge to help deliver this most British 'end of the pier' entertainment format to a US audience.

This was panto, LA style, which entertained generations from children to grandparents.

It was an enormous success. LA lapped it up. Actors who appeared in their shows down the years included, wait for it, pop sensation Ariana Grande (who was just enchanting as Snow White), *Dallas* icon Morgan Fairchild, Disney star Olivia Holt and American actress Lauren Taylor.

I was thoroughly absorbed in the world of entertainment. I was meeting the most amazing people and forming new friendships.

One friend is Sophie Dashwood, who I first met during these exciting times. Sophie had dated Motown legend, Lionel Richie.

The former Commodore's lead singer is, of course, one of the world's most successful recording artists of all time with record sales surpassing 100 million worldwide. His duet with fellow Motown icon Diane Ross "Endless Love," became one of the biggest hits around the world. He co-wrote the 1985 charity single "We Are the World" with Michael Jackson, which sold over 20 million copies.

I attended his concert in Cardiff as Sophie and Lionel's guest at the Motorpoint Arena in 2015. We all chatted backstage before the show. What a lovely guy he was; not at all affected by his fame as we chatted casually like old friends. I couldn't help thinking that this guy was probably treating me with as much civility as he would have shown to Diana Ross, Michael Jackson, or any of the other superstars he had encountered. It was a lovely lesson in how to treat people with dignity and good grace – even when you have never met before.

It was a lesson I have seen in other international stars.

Another good friend is Karen Struel-White, the daughter of former Swansea City Football Club chairman Malcolm Struel. Karen is a well-known producer and talent agent, known for

168

The Queen's Wrist and *Mr Easy Guy* (2010). Her other credits include *WAG: The Musical!*

Karen introduced me to Sir Ian McKellen at one private theatre event, with whom we enjoyed a memorable evening.

Sir Ian is an icon of British theatre whose career includes Shakespearean roles, modern theatre, fantasy and science fiction. He has received numerous awards and nominations for two Academy Awards, five Prime time Emmy Awards, and four BAFTAs. He turned out to be charming and engaging company.

Coldplay's Chris Martin had displayed similar qualities when I met him whilst I was advising recording studio owners at Primrose Hill, London. Chris was recording there at the time.

Acting and producing were certainly professionally fulfilling. The opportunities to rub shoulders with stars of the stage and screen, and giants of the music scene were also obviously extremely exciting, but also taught me many important lessons about people skills. The stars I remember with most affection – like Lionel Richie, George Michael, and Sir Ian, had time for people.

Their fame went before them but, in my experience, that did not prevent them from acting with dignity and good manners. These were true gentlemen, from whom I learned much from our brief encounters.

Yet again, these were great times. Sure, good fortune had played its part along the way but, as you may realise by now, you have to make your own luck at times.

Seize those moments. Create those moments. It's that "time and chance" factor again, isn't it? Hard work, innovation, self-belief, surrounding yourself with good people who share your drive, and building relationships. These are the key to success in any area. Treat people with dignity at all levels.

A new career had opened for me, and I was enjoying life to the full. My hobby had once again turned into my job. Life was rich and rewarding. Good times lay ahead for the foreseeable future.

Or did they?

My Biggest Battle

Party invites continued to land at my door thick and fast, along with offers to collaborate on new theatre projects and offers of acting roles. However, Thursday 14 July 2016 was a day to which I was looking forward with eagerness.

A sporting event to enjoy away from all the razzamatazz. England was set to face Pakistan in the opening Test Match at Lords. Alastair Cook and Joe Root were set to feature for England. For the tourists, Misbah-ul-Haq would provide stiff resistance with the bat, while I was also looking forward to enjoying leg-spinner Yasir Shah with the ball in his hands.

Located in St John's Wood, London NW8, Lords is one of my favourite sporting venues and almost certainly my favourite cricket ground. It is steeped in history. The venue celebrated its 200th anniversary in 2014. Parts of the ground enjoy listed building status; such is its splendour and magnificence. It is owned by Marylebone Cricket Club (the MCC) and is also home to the world's oldest sporting museum.

The historic venue also features a plaque which I purchased in 2021 for inclusion on the famous Father Time Wall, which celebrates the 100 Greatest Milestones to ever take place at the ground. Surrounded by thousands of personalised supporter plaques, it gives cricket fans the chance to feature on the wall alongside their cricketing heroes. My plaque simply reads "Jonathan Power and family, Cardiff, Glam. Love Lords." Part of my legacy for the days when I am no longer 'at the crease' so to speak.

On a sunny day with a cold beer in hand, a packed Lords is hard to beat, especially on the opening morning of a Test Match when the venue bristles with anticipation. The MCC members would look splendid in their famous red and yellow ties, recognised the world over and affectionately referred to as "egg and bacon." Little wonder that the venue is known as The Home of Cricket.

The visitors opened the batting, having won the toss to decide who would bat first and who would field. Pakistan made 339, with Misbah-ul-Haq scoring 114. Chris Woakes returned impressive bowling figures of 6 for 70.

I enjoyed all this sitting with friends at the Nursery End of the ground. At the end of a splendid day of cricket, there was time for a quick final beer before heading back to my Chelsea apartment. I would return to Cardiff the following day. This had been the common format for many trips to London over the years.

As I arranged myself for an evening back at the flat, I cleaned my teeth ahead of retiring for the night. The usual night-time ritual I guess.

To my surprise, I noticed a strange appearance in my reflection in the bathroom mirror. A lump had appeared on the side of my neck.

I tried not to think about this strange growth as I hit the sack but, on waking the following morning, the lump was still there. I hadn't recalled seeing it the previous morning. I decided to have it checked out back in Cardiff.

Despite not being a regular attendee at my doctor's surgery, my GP agreed to see me straight away.

Immediately, Dr Sian Salek noticed the strange growth and asked how long it had been visible.

After an initial examination, she was on the phone to the Emergency Unit at the University Hospital of Wales, located in Heath, Cardiff. She made an immediate referral to the unit. Alarm bells began to ring in my head.

At the hospital, it was decided that I should begin a week's course of antibiotics. I think the staff thought the growth could simply be a reaction to recent dental surgery. If the growth remained in place after this medication, I was to return to my GP.

I am afraid to report that the antibiotics made no impact on the strange growth, and Dr Salek therefore referred me to the ear, nose and throat (ENT) specialists back at the hospital.

Events seemed to move at pace, and before long I found

myself in the company of Mr David Owens. David was an authority in his field with a strong reputation for expertise in the diagnosis, evaluation, and management of diseases of the head and neck.

Mr Owens had been a consultant ENT surgeon at the University Hospital of Wales since 2011. He graduated in Leicester and gained postgraduate ENT training in Wales. He sat on the specialist advisory committee for ENT at the Royal College of Surgeons of Edinburgh and was the Regional Advisor for Wales at ENTUK Council.

Doctors who specialise in this area are called otorhinolaryngologists, otolaryngologists, head and neck surgeons, or ENT surgeons or physicians, I was to discover. I was in good hands for sure.

During my initial consultation, Mr Owens said that he would be referring me for a biopsy and further investigation, as he calmly explained that in his professional opinion, the growth was likely to be cancerous.

I can hear his words to this day.

"In my professional opinion….," though the bulk of the rest of his commentary remains a total blur.

I felt my world had collapsed around me.

I was only 52 years of age and, despite a busy life in a high-profile environment I had enjoyed reasonable fitness and good health. I had given up smoking earlier that year and even the finer things in life such as fine foods and liquid lunches had only been taken in moderation, I told myself.

'Shock' doesn't even come close.

The next few weeks positively raced by. Further meetings, diagnosis, consultations, and scans…. all simply confirmed the worst.

The C-word.

At 52 years of age.

The tumour which had formed on my neck required immediate removal. I was prepared to pay for private treatment in the hope of speeding matters up. Mr Owens advised though, that

172

this was unlikely to lead to a quicker outcome and I was only likely to end back referred to him anyway. The things you learn, eh?

David and I built up a wonderful rapport. Members of his team were also a great source of strength as I faced an uncertain future. The bitterest pill I ever had to swallow.

Despite my trust in Mr Owens and his colleagues, and in a state of panic following my first consultation, on hearing this terrible news I even visited Harley Street, but made no progress in the absence of a formal referral.

I decided that I had to place my trust in Mr Owens' experienced and skilled hands and ignored the advice of keyboard warriors and a thousand websites. It was the only way to remain sane.

From the first delivery that day at Lords, to the day of my operation on 31st August, the time flashed by in the blink of an eye. Faster than the bowling of Jimmy Anderson even.

It was a terrifying time, though. I was scared for myself, desperate for my family and uncertain about the future. There had been so much to look forward to; holidays with Emma, cricket tours, Millie growing up. Would I even get to walk my precious daughter down the aisle? Grandchildren? Clouds surrounded me; engulfed me. There seemed no light at the end of this unexpected tunnel.

Emma and I took the view that we would try to protect Millie from exposure to this nightmare as far as we possibly could. Yes, she knew things were going on, but it was important that she lived her life without the pressure that this ruddy cancerous growth had brought us all. Millie was only 12 at the time. An important age: an awkward age even, as she faced up to high school and life as a teenager. GCSEs. A Levels, Universities to choose. Millie had her entire future ahead of her.

Problem was, would that future include me?

We restricted the news to immediate family. Not even my parents knew at first.

173

30 August 2016.

The day before my operation. I met the whole cancer care team, one after another. In my professional life I had been proud of my ability to create and sustain teams of the best performers. This time the team had been built for me, though I could not have hand-picked a better line-up.

A large group of practitioners had been assembled to take care of me. Larger than I expected if truth be told. Pre and post-cancer care teams, dieticians and even a psychologist. I don't recall a goalkeeping coach but who knows, I may have missed that one!

I was advised that Dr Mererid Evans would become my clinical oncologist. Her specialism was in the management of patients with head and neck cancer. Like I say, I was in expert hands.

Notwithstanding these turbulent times, I tried to remain my usual self. I tried to retain a positive mindset and did my best to manage my illness with confidence. Some would say I was quite cavalier about it all. "How do you stay so upbeat?" they said.

Sleep in the afternoon helped conserve my energy levels. My condition was serious, I knew that, but my natural optimism and self-belief kicked in to help me survive the storms.

Well, sometimes anyway.

Maybe this was all my way of coping. Was I living 'behind a painted smile' through all this? I had no precedent. Life in the fast line had not prepared me for this.

The day of the operation dawned. The procedure could last a few hours, they said. I assumed my position on the operating table. The skilled team stood by, as an injection sent me to the land of nod.

It was out of my hands now.

***

Apparently, the operation did not exactly go to plan. During the procedure I had woken and was coughing up blood. A second injection returned me to my slumber.

Emma waited anxiously in a nearby room, her anguish growing as the hours passed. All seven of them in total.

Once the operation was eventually complete, the staff transferred me to a ward where I was to rest and recover. I tried to take it easy but, reverting to type, I also found the energy to check out the football transfer gossip on my mobile phone. Some things just never change, do they? Fancy putting me to sleep on transfer deadline day!

My spirits took another dip the following day though, as Mr Owens met up with me to discuss progress.

This turned out to be a difficult dialogue as he revealed to me that the cancer within the tumour had spread. He recommended follow-up treatment which would feature radiotherapy and chemotherapy.

As you might appreciate this was not welcome news. Wrongly, I had convinced myself that they would simply cut the tumour out and I would be up and running in no time, dabbling my fingers into all the usual business opportunities and ventures that I liked to enjoy.

I was invited to attend Velindre Hospital – a specialist facility caring for cancer patients in Whitchurch, Cardiff – where oncologist Dr Mererid Evans outlined the next steps.

Her plans were to include two sessions of chemotherapy and 30 sessions of radiotherapy. My immune system was expected to take a big hit. It would be like being hit by a truck. The truck would reverse back over you too.

The treatment offered the best chance of ensuring that any remaining cancer cells would be wiped out. I had little choice but to go ahead with this uncomfortable remedy and just hope that it worked. It was a battle I simply had to face.

It would be my biggest battle.

September 2016.

Another month had passed. Another hospital. This time I would be out at Llandough, in the Vale of Glamorgan. Ordinarily, the Vale of Glamorgan is a beautiful part of Wales. Sharing a border with the capital, it is home to the most southerly point of Wales with a stunning coast, seaside resorts, chocolate box villages and sweeping areas of beautiful rural charm.

This would be no relaxing break in the countryside though. As the forthcoming treatment of radiotherapy would affect my ability to eat, a feeding tube was inserted to provide for my nutritional needs. The treatment would affect my ability to maintain weight and gain any nutrition. The tube was fed into my stomach through the abdominal wall, a method known as a percutaneous endoscopic gastrostomy (PEG) tube. Normal eating and drinking would not be possible.

No Saturday night curries for me then.

I could also expect unpleasant side effects from the arduous radiotherapy treatment that was about to follow.

Open sores in my mouth and throat. Ulcers, dry mouth, difficulty in swallowing, nausea, change in taste, tooth decay and swelling in the gums, throat and neck.

Just before the commencement of treatment, the full oncology team met with me. Becky Bailey, Dr Evans' trusted assistant, joined members of the dietary team to prepare me for the difficult times ahead and provide their expert advice and support.

The dietary advice before my treatment recommended a full-fat diet. Cakes for breakfast and even milky coffee. Weight gain would be an important factor in preparing me for the forthcoming treatment – which would see me drastically lose weight.

I was also fitted with a mask – sometimes called a mould, head shell or cast. The device would keep my head and neck still. It was important that my head and neck remained in the same position, to help ensure that the radiotherapy treatment was as accurate and effective as possible. It could be extremely claustrophobic.

Other 'highlights' included a permanent ink mark on my chest to help the radiographer deliver the gruelling radiotherapy treatment with precision.

When the treatment started, I had to lie in the same position on a couch below the radiotherapy machine. Each lasted up to 20 minutes, leaving me exhausted. I would sleep for 18 hours a day at times. Emma fed me a variety of 'shakes' via the PEG tube as I could no longer eat properly. I had no strength to feed myself. I was that weak.

It was awful. Just awful.

At the end of six weeks of treatment for both radiotherapy and chemotherapy, I was out on my feet. I was also on 40 tablets a day.

40.

If this was what the treatment felt like, how would the actual illness have felt I wondered?

Sometimes, I could barely sit up or raise myself in my bed. It was a huge effort to even take a shower. I had always taken a pride in my appearance since my days as a fashion-conscious teenager, but this malarkey just seemed to drain all life and energy from me. As my immune system deteriorated, long stays back in hospital became the norm.

Inevitably during such dark days, one's thoughts turn to "what might be."

I even thought about the end.

My own mortality was not something on which I had focussed previously.

Spike Milligan had said, "I don't mind dying. I just don't want to be there when it happens." I guess that had been my philosophy up to now.

The long, dark, agonising hours in a hospital bed whilst being desperately ill can suck the spirit from the liveliest of souls though. The optimism which had characterised my days as an entrepreneur and advisor to the stars became a distant memory. Now a shadow of my former self I found myself addressing the thought of my own passing. I had to contemplate a scenario where Mrs E. Power could become a widow. I owed her that.

Not to mention a certain Miss M. Power.

I raised the topic with Emma one day at Velindre as I lay desperately ill. I was now fighting to stay alive. It was probably the lowest point of my illness. The lowest of my life, even.

But......

Cast your eyes back a few paragraphs.

"....... where Mrs E. Power could become a widow."

"Could."

Not would.

Whose choice would that be?

The medical team were doing all that they could. I even took comfort from prayer at times (not an area I had explored with great conviction in the past) but, in my heart of hearts I knew that the answer really only lay in the hands of one person.

Mr J. Power would have to dig deep. Really deep, to a level unknown before.

He would have to draw on resources that he may not have believed existed. A great life still lay ahead of him, potentially. He would have to fight for the right to enjoy that life. To be happy with Emma and Millie. I asked myself if I was up to the test. Was I about to surrender my bat to this demon bowler they call cancer, or dig in, repelling each aggressive delivery with steel, nerve, grit, and determination?

I would have to duck his bouncers and grin back at him from beneath my MCC helmet. I would need some luck along the way but, not for the first time in my life, I would have to make my own luck.

My toughest test but my easiest choice.

I was up for the fight. Ready to go again.

The road to recovery would be long and arduous. I had been on the 'highway to hell' long enough though and I was ready to fight. Weak, underweight, and lifeless, I searched deep within myself for the strength I would need. I thought about Emma, about Millie, about cricket in the sun and football in the rain.

Chips in Caroline Street and cold lager from a beer garden. I clung to a future my family deserved. Gritted my teeth to face the toughest test.

Time passed slowly. The long and painful treatment took its effect. I remember Mr Owens saying that the form of cancer which affected me could potentially be treatable and even be capable of being cured.

This chink of light came during an awfully long, dark tunnel indeed, yet it brought music to my ears. A faint note of optimism along a bleak and often despairing journey. I metaphorically slammed the aggressive bowler for four, through a lush outfield!

As my recovery began to unfold, I spent time at home reflecting on these toughest of trials. I had been dropped into a nightmare scenario for which I was ill-prepared. The treatment had been agonising, with the first chemotherapy session taking up an entire day and night. That was on 2nd October 2016, followed by radiotherapy the very next day. Radiotherapy continued deep into November, which although was a day we felt able to welcome, it still heralded the start of a long and difficult journey.

Regular meetings with the post-cancer team ensured that my progress towards recovery over the coming months and even years, was carefully monitored.

I expect it sounds like something of a happy ending doesn't it and yes, we were pleased that the darkest days seemed behind me at last. I was driven by results and outcomes though. Always have been. Time lay so heavy on my hands as the physical pain of my illness and treatment gave way to emotional and psychological anguish. Why was my full recovery taking so long? Hadn't I done my bit by now? My mood began to change as the trauma I had faced continued to overwhelm my spirits. The gift which just kept on giving.

I admit that never once had I asked, "Why me?" though my frustration grew. I would occasionally find myself in floods of tears for no tangible reason. I tried to 'force' my recovery I suppose, which is simply a fool's game. Patience and humility were what were needed here, but I struggled to find either.

179

Often during consultation sessions with Mr Owens in those ensuing years, I would break down in floods of tears. My emotions were all at sea for reasons I was unable to explain. The long journey was becoming the 'road to nowhere.'

Was it relief from a lucky escape? Had I been 'spared' or was the reason less mysterious – mere frustration and boredom borne from time spent in my sick bed and on the hospital ward? I should have been ready to face the future with new hope, but something kept holding me back. As if the cancer was still clinging to some dark corner of my soul, determined to exert its ongoing influence over my persona and demeanour. Even when I was given the all clear on 24 January 2017, the emotional outbursts continued to surround me, overwhelming me, time after time.

Drawing upon his many years of experience, Mr Owens explained how, for many people who had encountered success in life, their road to recovery could coincide with a degree of emotional trauma. The path to recovery was a complex one, he explained, with twists and turns aplenty. The emotional journey was almost as arduous as the physical one I discovered. Long after the "Get Well Soon" cards had been taken down from my hospital ward, the unseen spectres would continue to haunt me.

It was also important that I avoided any stress during this time as well - throughout my recovery and beyond. My fragile metabolism and inner self were simply not ready to face the demands of work projects, business engagements or anything resembling the roles I had performed in the past. Rest and recuperation were to be the order of the day.

For a guy like me used to a fast-paced life, this was another bitter pill to swallow. I was determined to learn my lesson though, as I stepped off the gas for as long as it would take. Time would be the only healer here and I would gain little from trying to force the pace. Indeed, I would probably do more harm than good. Like a footballer who comes back before he really is match fit, I had to stay on the treatment table until I was emotionally and physically recovered, ready to cross that whitewash again.

This could take years, I thought.

Mr Owens never held back in his support for me and referred me to a specialist psychologist. Janice Rees was experienced in supporting cancer patients. Her care and compassion helped me navigate the dark corners and corridors my mind inhabited during those uncertain times. I was experiencing a kind of post-trauma stress disorder, she explained. Not uncommon in cases such as mine.

It was five long years before I was eventually strong enough to really pick up the pieces again. Years of consultation, advice and support. My entire post-cancer care team had carried me through it, often when I felt unable to face the future. No matter how determined I was to pull myself through it, I could not have made it without their professional and personal care and attention.

Thanks guys.

Mr Owens assured me that, no matter what the future would bring he would remain just a phone call away. My life had experienced a trauma which could change me forever.

I would slowly continue to seek out new opportunities and chances. After all, life was there to be lived for us again. A fascinating career had brought me into contact with some wonderful people. Knights of the Realm who would inspire with their dignity and drive. Professional athletes with a hunger for success. Stars of the stage and screen alongside ordinary guys who'd shaped my enthusiasm. Family and friends who had inspired and encouraged me. You have met many of them on these pages. I had enjoyed the trappings of success brought from hard work. It had certainly been a life worth living.

I hope that this chapter has shown you a glimpse that even in the darkest hours, there remains a place for optimism and positive thought. Make your own luck, with drive and determination.

I owe Mr Owens, Mererid Evans and Janice Rees an enormous debt, alongside the rest of the NHS. I may never really understand and appreciate the care I received, though I try.

By 2022, I am pleased to say that I found myself fit and well and able to take regular exercise. Cricket trips to the West Indies and Australia have been among the highlights of my travels since recovering from my illness. I must exercise caution of course but, to all intents and purposes, my life is back on track.

My business interests these days encompass a property portfolio and, no doubt, other opportunities to keep me stimulated will continue to arise. Having enjoyed my time in the world of art and entertainment, I may also dip my toe back into those waters in due course, should the right opportunity manifest itself. Who knows what the future may deliver? My illness had taught me that.

Although I try not to dwell on the events of those five arduous years, brought on by illness, my take on life is quite different these days. I remain a man of business enterprise but these days, my primary focus lies elsewhere.

Family life is rich and rewarding and my career is the gift which keeps on giving. Millie has blossomed to the brink of adulthood. Her ambitions lay in performing arts and the stage. She sits alongside Emma and I as we enjoy the top stars in concert or performing on stage.

We have enjoyed concerts by Placebo and My Chemical Romance. She was especially thrilled that I was able to help engineer an encounter with Ed Sheeran. He was really encouraging when she mentioned that she was looking to build a career in music.

I have been delighted to use my connections and experiences to introduce her to current household names like this. A memorable night at the 2022 Brit Awards saw us meet current stars of the music scene such as Sam Fender, Oli Sykes and Celeste.

Not a day passes when I don't look at Millie with pride, love, relief, and gratitude. Endless hours of exhausting treatment had left their mark on me for sure. Emotional scars which, in time, will heal.

They fade into the distance though when I hear Millie laugh or watch her smile. Days I might not have seen.

And no, Mrs E.Power is still not a widow.

My Top 10 Tips for Business Success

"The backbone of success is hard work, determination, good planning and perseverance." (Mia Hamm, retired professional US soccer player, two-time Olympic gold medallist, and two-time FIFA Women's World Cup champion.)

When the idea of writing this book first came to me, many thought it was a great idea.

That was all very well I suppose, but I wanted to leave a legacy to inspire others; to encourage youngsters to chase their dream or inspire existing high performers to go further and surpass themselves. To quote Mylene Klass, "they don't teach this at school. It's your attitude that counts, not your education."

I envisaged this book as much more than a good yarn; I wanted to offer business advice to the up-and-coming; to tease out and encourage the ambition and entrepreneurial spirit that lies within so many people.

It might even lie within you.

Hopefully, throughout the preceding pages, you have picked up some nuggets of advice and encouragement to inspire your dream. As I near the end of my odyssey though, let's see if we can gather some of these notions together. A blueprint for success.

Well, it worked for me.

1. Have a Plan

"A goal without a plan is just a wish." (Antoine de Saint-Exupéry. French writer, poet, aristocrat, journalist, and pioneering aviator.)

Really, I cannot overestimate the importance of this. Devise a business strategy. Write it down. Review and appraise it. Measure performance against it. Will it push you to success? What are your aims, goals, and objectives? Ask yourself, "what will success look like?"

By failing to plan you are planning to fail.

I realise this may all sound like business jargon, but this is the language of business. Get used to the vocabulary and embrace the culture.

Aim to achieve your goals no matter how large or small your venture might be.

2. Be Creative

"If you always do what you've always done, you'll always get what you've always got." (Henry Ford. American industrialist 1863 – 1947.)

Think outside the box. Don't be afraid to try new ideas.

Involve your team if you have one. Share your thoughts, encourage innovation, and reward enterprise. Dream big and dream new.

3. Be Different

"I don't care if I was a ditch-digger at a dollar a day, I'd want to do my job better than the fellow next to me. I'd want to be the best at whatever I do." (Branch Rickey: December 20, 1881 – December 9, 1965 – American baseball player and sports executive.)

Be ready to stand out from the crowd. Know your competition and seek out ways to be different. What's your USP (unique selling point)? Define it, exploit it. Maintain that competitive edge.

4. Be Flexible

"What we anticipate seldom occurs; what we least expect generally happens." (Benjamin Disraeli.)

No matter how well you plan, things may not always turn out as you expect. I have encountered enough twists and turns along the way to realise that. You must be flexible. Responsive to change. Your business must be able to think on its feet.

Embrace change. Don't be afraid to re-engineer your business to respond to new challenges or changes in the landscape you inhabit.

Take advantage of the opportunities this might create.

5. Be Resilient

"You can't start a fire, worrying about your little world falling apart." (Bruce Springsteen "Dancing in the Dark".)

Similarly, no matter how successful you become, there may still be setbacks along the way. Life has a habit of dealing you the odd low blow from time to time; the occasional bouncer that you failed to spot against the sight screens. A decision that doesn't go your way.

Learn from these. Don't dwell on them.

Stay strong in mind and retain your focus.

6. Work Hard. Work Harder. Work Harder Still.

"Unless commitment is made, there are only promises and hopes... but no plans." (Peter Drucker, management consultant, author, and educator.)

Be passionate about your business venture. If you can't show belief in your product, how do you expect to engage the rest of the world? Your confidence and enthusiasm will engage clients, supporters, and sponsors, creating opportunities. Making your own luck? If you like, yes, though think of it as preparing the ground. Get the soil conditions right and your crops will grow.

There is no shortcut to success. You must work hard.
I used to think nothing of working long hours.
24 Hours a day. 7 Days a week.

In an interview with a national newspaper, I once explained that if there were 48 hours in a single day, I would work them! It sounds a cliché but trust me, those pound notes don't grow on trees.

7. Team Play is the Best Play

"Football is like a piano; you need eight men to carry it and three who can play the damn thing." (Football boss, Bill Shankly.)

Build effective teams with complementary skills, experience, and strengths. Learn the importance of delegation. Empower your team. Create head space for yourself.

8. Surround Yourself with Positive People

"Blessed is the man who expects nothing, for he will never be disappointed." (Alexander Pope.)

Steer clear of negative people. You don't need them. Negativity is like jealousy, greed, or envy. It's just wasted energy.
Negative people will drag you down.
You know the type, could've; would've; should've.
I am not saying that you should not listen to cautious, responsible advice when contemplating difficult decisions but don't tell me what can't be done; tell me what *can* be done.
Mix with the do-ers; those that do and have done.

186

9. Be Confident!

"Between the optimist and the pessimist, the difference is droll. The optimist sees the doughnut, the pessimist, the hole." (Anon)

Set goals. Identify targets.

My single-mindedness when building my business gave me drive and energy which spread to my team. Confidence breeds confidence. It also breeds successful teams. It is highly infectious!

10. Keep a good Mindset. Be sharp!

"All work and no play, makes Jon a dull boy." (Adapted from James Howell's Proverbs, 1659.)

Make sure you build in rest. Take time out for yourself. Holidays, downtime, friends, and family. So important.

Maintain your health and fitness. That graveyard is full of people who thought they were indispensable.

***

These tips are my own, though I have deliberately included the thoughts of other eminent commentators, scholars, and practitioners. Never be too proud to learn from others.

After all, Disraeli, Henry Ford, and even Shanks knew a thing or two about wisdom, innovation, and success.

The concentrated thoughts of others are always worth studying, though great quotes are not where you find great wisdom.

"It's where you share this knowledge that counts." (Michael Joseph Farrelly.)

That's why I am sharing them with you.

You might think that some of these tips overlap. Repeat themselves even.

I believe though, that if you apply these principles then really, the only barrier to success is likely to come from within. Don't hold back on your potential.

Release those dreams.

Just go for it!

Epilogue

On retiring from my life as a financial advisor/agent, I knew that I would retain little contact with former clients and their representatives. They were great days, but they were over.

Or so I thought.

The office accommodation which I once occupied in Penarth, in the Vale of Glamorgan, which I kept on, has been converted to residential use now. My father lived there for a while.

We still receive correspondence sent to that address and Dad draws my attention to anything I need to see. Mostly it's copies of correspondence aimed at other parties, which no longer concerns me, or junk mail.

In July 2021 though, a letter arrived out of the blue. Dad felt I should be aware.

The letter concerned a critical illness policy that I had put in place for a former client some 20 years ago.

The correspondence stated that the policy was due to come to an end and I knew that it would still be possible for a claim to be made, should the right circumstances apply. I telephoned the former client.

To be honest, I was not even sure that he would remember me this far down the line. Names and faces slip from the memory with ease.

To his credit though, he did recall me. "How was I," he asked? Whilst he was kind enough to remember me, he had forgotten all about the policy itself despite still paying the premiums.

I reminded him about the policy. I explained that I was aware by reading a press article, of the profoundly serious illness that he had suffered, and that a successful claim could be anticipated.

I had always prided myself on the service I provided to my clients. It was simply in my nature to go the extra mile, to add the personal touch or offer that extra helping hand if I could. It was just my business ethic. Clients respected this and it paid dividends.

The famous figure on the other end of the call was genuinely moved. Not only had I kept up to date with the policy, but I had shown compassion in ringing him directly. I knew his circumstances. I knew a claim could succeed. Had I ignored the letter, the former client would have been none the wiser and the policy would have simply come to an end.

The earning potential of some of the stars I advised was enormous, but it doesn't last forever. You are a long-time retired. Bills still must be paid. Kids need shoes. Real life can be expensive. Events can throw off your spending plans. I knew the backstory of my former client.

It was a moving exchange. 14 years on from my days in the financial sector, I still remained a confidant to this household name. The claim would make an enormous difference to his difficult, personal circumstances. We both knew this.

My father's intervention in my professional life had continued to shape my decisions. Dad was a significant influence in the first chapter of this book and here he was at the end. My parents continue to drive, motivate and inspire me with the choices they made for me. "Make things happen," they said. "Make things happen."

This story is a fitting postscript to this book. My career has been a successful one. Clients had been giants from the world of sport and entertainment. Many have become friends. The work ethic inspired by my parents continued to serve me well. Doubters had been proved wrong.

I knew that the tough circumstances of my former client would improve greatly because of this windfall, which I had created for him with careful advice and long-term planning. His life would turn around now.

All because of a phone call.

Oh, the value of the successful claim by the way?

One million pounds.

About the Authors

Jonathan Power is the ultimate example of a local boy made good.

From modest Pembrokeshire beginnings, this title takes us on his remarkable journey.

Uninspired by schoolteachers, and written off by others, his story is one of achievement, ambition, and results. Jonathon rubs shoulders with the stars throughout this illuminating narrative.

His story will inspire anyone with a dream. Jon's business strategy is based on enterprise, initiative, and a remarkable approach to relationship building which has taken him to the top of his profession.

Jonathan Power lives in Cardiff with his wife Emma and daughter Millie.

David Collins has written on the Welsh sporting, cultural and social scene for many years.

His numerous titles display his passion for football in Wales and beyond.

Currently operating across a range of bilingual, digital platforms, media channels, and hard copy publications, David is an accredited Dataco media representative, recognised by the Premier League, EFL, and on the international stage. David is now using his experience to inspire and mentor aspiring young sports writers at a clutch of UK universities.

David and Jon are also former football teammates, though perhaps the less said about that the better.